NATIONS OF THE WORLD

RUSSIA

Neil Wilson

RAINTREE
STECK-VAUGHN
PUBLISHERS

A Harcourt Company

Austin   New York
www.steck-vaughn.com

Steck-Vaughn Company

First published 2001 by Raintree Steck-Vaughn Publishers,
an imprint of Steck-Vaughn Company.
Copyright © 2001 Brown Partworks Limited.

Library of Congress Cataloging-in-Publication Data

Wilson, Neil, 1959–
    Russia / Neil Wilson.
       p. cm — (Nations of the world).
    Includes bibliographical references and index.
    ISBN 0-7398-1281-5
     1. Russia-Juvenile literature. [1.Russia]   I. Title.
II. Nations of the world (Austin, Tex.)
DK510.23.W55 2000
947--dc21

                  00–039027
                  CIP

Printed and bound in the United States
1 2 3 4 5 6 7 8 9 0   05 04 03 02 01 00

Brown Partworks Limited
Editor: Robert Anderson
Designer: Joan Curtis
Cartographers: William Le Bihan and
   Colin Woodman
Picture Researcher: Brenda Clynch
Editorial Assistant: Roland Ellis
Indexer: Kay Ollerenshaw

Raintree Steck-Vaughn
Publishing Director: Walter Kossmann
Art Director: Max Brinkmann

Front cover: Nevsky Prospekt, St. Petersburg (background); icon showing Saint Cyril (top left); onion domes of St. Basil's Cathedral, Moscow
Title page: silver-domed church in the Moscow region

Contents

Foreword

Since ancient times, people have gathered together in communities where they could share and trade resources and strive to build a safe and happy environment. Gradually, as populations grew and societies became more complex, communities expanded to become nations—groups of people who felt sufficiently bound by a common heritage to work together for a shared future.

Land has usually played an important role in defining a nation. People have a natural affection for the landscape in which they grew up. They are proud of its natural beauties—the mountains, rivers, and forests—and of the towns and cities that flourish there. People are proud, too, of their nation's history—the shared struggles and achievements that have shaped the way they live today.

Religion, culture, race, and lifestyle, too, have sometimes played a role in fostering a nation's identity. Often, though, a nation includes people of different races, beliefs, and customs. Many have come from distant countries, and some want to preserve their traditional lifestyles. Nations have rarely been fixed, unchanging things, either territorially or racially. Throughout history, borders have altered, often under the pressure of war, and people have migrated across the globe in search of a new life or of new land or because they are fleeing from oppression or disaster. The world's nations are still changing today: Some nations are breaking up and new nations are forming.

Russia began its history as a Slavic federation in eastern Europe. Over the centuries, its rulers, the czars, built Russia into a mighty empire that stretched the length of Asia. Many peoples of varied beliefs and ethnicities came to be included in the empire, but the Russian people remained dominant. In the 20th century, Russia's communist rulers tried to unify this diverse country under the banner of communism, often riding roughshod over the rights of minority peoples. As the Russian Federation, the country began to build a new democratic nation, but has still to come to terms with its ethnic complexity.

Introduction

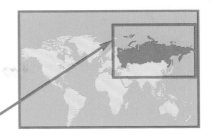

RUSSIA

Zdrastvuitye—"hello" and welcome to Russia, the largest country in the world. Its huge area contains many different landscapes; from vast, empty plains to dark, dense forests. Its many cities vary from old walled towns with onion-domed cathedrals to sprawling, smoky metropolises.

Russia is also culturally diverse, its ancient name bringing to mind some of the world's greatest authors and musicians, including the writer Lev (Leo) Tolstoy and the composer Pyotr Tchaikovsky. Yet Russia's name also brings to mind some of the world's most feared and hated rulers, including the czar, or emperor, Ivan the Terrible and the communist dictator Joseph Stalin.

Russia stretches almost halfway around the Northern Hemisphere. One part of Russia is in Europe and is generally referred to as European Russia, but a larger part is in Asia. The country's most easterly point is Big Diomede Island in the Bering Strait, only 2.5 miles (4 km) from the United States' Little Diomede Island.

Russia's most westerly point is the city of Kaliningrad, standing on a small wedge of Russian territory sandwiched between Poland and Lithuania in Europe. The country stretches south from the Arctic Circle to the deserts of Central Asia and China. In total, Russia covers an area almost twice the size of the United States and accounts for almost one-eighth of the Earth's land area.

St. Basil's Cathedral in Moscow's Red Square is famous for its colorful onion-shaped domes. Built between 1555 and 1560, it is today a museum.

FACT FILE

● From 1922 to 1991, Russia was the leading member of the Union of Soviet Socialist Republics (USSR), or Soviet Union.

● Russia is so big that it spans 11 time zones: When it is midnight in Kaliningrad, it is 10 A.M. in Kamchatka in the east.

● The world's coldest inhabited place is found in Russia. The town of Verkhoyansk, in northeastern Siberia, records temperatures as low as -96°F (-71°C).

● From east to west, the country has a maximum extent of some 4,800 miles (7,700 km)—about twice the breadth of the United States.

РОССИЯ

(Right) This is the Russian word for "Russia" written in the Cyrillic alphabet.

Russia has played a major part in the shaping of today's world. The Russian Revolution of 1917 led to the formation of the Union of Soviet Socialist Republics (USSR), or the Soviet Union for short, the world's first communist nation.

The USSR included Russia as well as neighboring countries that had long formed part of the Russian empire. Russia, however, was the leading member of the union. Military rivalry between the USSR and the United States after World War II (1939–1945) caused a long period of international tension, often called the Cold War. Today, Russia has entered a period of turbulence and uncertainty, from which it is still struggling to free itself.

In 1991, the tricolor (three-striped flag), first used in 1799, was readopted as the national flag.

NAME, CURRENCY, FLAG, AND ANTHEM

Russia's official name is the Russian Federation—*Rossiyskaya Federatsiya* in Russian. It took this name in 1991, when many territories that had previously been part of the Soviet Union became independent countries. Today, the Russian Federation includes independent areas that usually have large non-Russian minorities; they are often referred to as the "ethnic" or "minority" republics. Russia's capital is the ancient city of Moscow, known as *Moskva* in Russian.

Owing to Russia's unpredictable economy, the value of Russia's currency, the ruble, can fluctuate wildly. Although it is illegal, many people prefer to be paid in U.S. dollars.

The Russian currency is the ruble, which is officially divided into 100 kopecks. The country's national flag has three horizontal bands of white, blue, and red. It was used from 1799 until the 1917 Revolution and reintroduced in 1991.

The stirring Russian national anthem has no words. The anthem's music is taken from an opera by the 19th-century Russian composer Mikhail Glinka.

POPULATION DENSITY

Most of Russia's population lives in the far west of the country, particularly around the cities of Moscow and St. Petersburg. East of the Ural Mountains, the vast Siberian plains are only sparsely populated. The exceptions are the industrial heartlands north of Omsk and a narrow strip of territory in the far east around the port of Vladivostok.

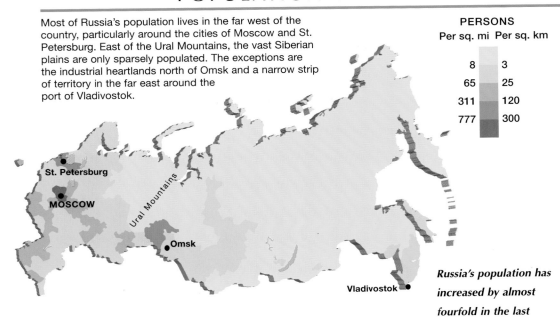

PERSONS

Per sq. mi	Per sq. km
8	3
65	25
311	120
777	300

Russia's population has increased by almost fourfold in the last 200 years. However, experts predict that it will fall sharply over the coming decades.

PEOPLE AND LANGUAGES

The Russian Federation has a population of almost 150 million, with an average population density of 23 people per square mile (8.7 people per sq. km). This statistic is misleading, as about four-fifths of the population lives west of the Ural Mountains in European Russia. The huge expanse of Siberia, in the east, is very sparsely populated.

Ethnic Russians—the original inhabitants of Kievan Rus' (*see* pp. 53–55)—make up four-fifths of the total population. Russia is also home, however, to more than a hundred other nationalities, including Ukrainians and Belorussians in the west; Ossetians, Chechens, and Ingushetians in the Caucasus; Tatars and Bashkirs in the central steppes; and Buryats, Yakuts, and Samoyeds in Siberia.

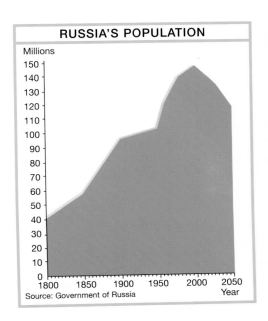

RUSSIA'S POPULATION

Millions

Source: Government of Russia

Year

POPULATION BY AGE

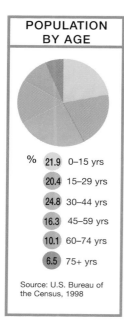

%	
21.9	0–15 yrs
20.4	15–29 yrs
24.8	30–44 yrs
16.3	45–59 yrs
10.1	60–74 yrs
6.5	75+ yrs

Source: U.S. Bureau of the Census, 1998

The charts above and below show how Russia's population divides by age, ethnicity, and religion.

WHERE DOES RUSSIA'S POPULATION LIVE?

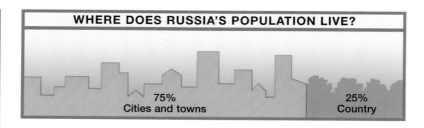

75%
Cities and towns

25%
Country

Many of these peoples have their own republic or independent territory as part of the Russian Federation.

The official language is Russian, which is written using the 32-letter Cyrillic alphabet. Based on the Greek and Hebrew alphabets, the Cyrillic alphabet was invented by Saint Cyril and Saint Methodius, Christian missionaries to Russia and nearby countries in the ninth century.

There are dozens of other languages spoken by minority peoples. These include the Turkic languages spoken by the Tatar, Chuvash, Bashkir, and Yakut peoples; the Indo-European languages used by the Ukrainian, Belorussian, Ossetian, and Armenian minorities; the Komi, Nentsy, and Khanty languages of the northern Siberian peoples; and the Cherkess, Chechen-Ingush, and Lezgian tongues of the Caucasus region.

ETHNIC COMPOSITION

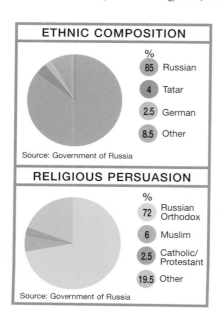

%	
85	Russian
4	Tatar
2.5	German
8.5	Other

Source: Government of Russia

RELIGIOUS PERSUASION

%	
72	Russian Orthodox
6	Muslim
2.5	Catholic/ Protestant
19.5	Other

Source: Government of Russia

Russia's Symbols

The symbol of the old Russian empire was a double-headed eagle. There were once bronze eagles on top of the Kremlin towers in Moscow, but after the Russian Revolution in 1917, they were replaced with red stars, a popular communist emblem that was also the badge of the Red Army. The hammer and sickle were adopted as the state symbol of the USSR. The sickle represented farm laborers; the hammer was for factory workers. Russia as a country is often symbolized by a brown bear, a common inhabitant of the Russian forests.

Russia has no official religion. The Soviet regime tried to eradicate religion by closing churches, confiscating church property, and persecuting priests. Since 1991, and the return of religious freedom, Russia's ancient Christian church—the Russian Orthodox church—has recovered and now has about 110 million members. Many churches and cathedrals, which had been neglected, destroyed, or used for non-religious purposes under communism, are now being restored or rebuilt.

There are around nine million Muslims, living mainly in the republics of Tatarstan and Bashkortostan and in the Caucasus region. Some of the native peoples of northern Siberia are shamanists—shamanism is a religion of nature spirits. In the republics along the Mongolian and Chinese border are peoples who follow Tibetan Buddhism. Small communities of Jews, Catholics, and Protestants are spread throughout the federation.

Hello, Anna Borisovna!

Russians usually have three names: a first name, a middle name based on their father's first name, or patronymic, and a family name. There are two forms of a patronymic— a woman's patronymic ends with "-ovna," and a man's with "-vich." Russians often address each other using both first name and patronymic—for example, Anna Borisovna ("Anna, daughter of Boris") and Pavel Nikolaevich ("Pavel, son of Nikolay").

Writing Russian Proper Names and Words

In this book, Russian names and words are written not using the Cyrillic alphabet, but using an English version of Cyrillic. This process of representing a language written using one alphabet with the alphabet used by another is called transliteration.

There are several systems currently in use for transliterating Russian using the Roman alphabet. This book generally uses a method recommended by the U.S. Library of Congress.

Sometimes, however, place-names and other words are so well known using another system that this form is used instead—for example, Moscow (Russia's capital), Baikal (a lake in Siberia), and ruble (the currency).

Similarly, well-known figures from Russia's history are written using their English forms. The famous Russian czar who started the Russian empire is Peter, not *Piotr*, the Great, and the Russian saint is Basil, not *Vasil*.

Land and Cities

"You can take the whole of the United States...and set it down in the middle of Siberia without touching anywhere the boundaries of the latter's territory..."

George Kennan, in *Siberia and the Exile System*, 1891

Russia's most outstanding geographical feature is its size. Stretching for just under 5,000 miles (8,000 km) from the Gulf of Finland in the west to the Bering Strait in the east, it occupies one-quarter of the Eurasian landmass (the combined continents of Europe and Asia). In total, Russia encompasses an area of 6,592,800 square miles (17,075,400 sq. km)—about 1.8 times the area of the United States, including Alaska.

Russia shares its borders with 13 other countries. To the west are Ukraine, Belarus, Latvia, Estonia, Lithuania, Finland, and Norway, while to the south are North Korea, China, Mongolia, Kazakhstan, Azerbaijan, and Georgia. The western borders are largely unprotected by geographic barriers such as rivers or mountains. Those to the south, however, are fenced by towering mountains, desolate steppes, or grasslands, and vast inland seas.

The remainder of Russia's borders are washed by cold, icy seas—by the Arctic Ocean in the north and by the northern Pacific in the east. In the northwest, the Gulf of Finland—an arm of the Baltic Sea—gives Russia valuable access to the ports of northern Europe.

Within Russia's vast territory are a wide range of landscapes. There are the snowy forests of Siberia and the glacier-capped peaks of the Caucasus Mountains, the rolling wheatfields around the Volga River and the smoldering volcanoes of the Kamchatka Peninsula.

FACT FILE

- Russia's—and Europe's—highest point is at the top of Mount Elbrus, an extinct volcano in the Caucasus Mountains. It rises to 18,510 feet (5,642 m).

- The lowest point is the Caspian Sea, the surface of which is 92 feet (28 m) below sea level.

- Europe's two largest lakes are in Russia—Lake Ladoga (6,835 sq. mi or 17,703 sq. km) and Lake Onega (3,710 sq. mi or 9,609 sq. km).

- In 1992, Russian scientists estimated that 15 percent of Russia's land was "ecologically unsafe" owing to the high levels of pollution.

A herdsman watches over his reindeer in Siberia. Despite being covered with snow for two-thirds of the year, the region supports large numbers of livestock.

TERRAIN

Russia encompasses a huge variety of landforms and landscapes. North to south the country passes through four major landscape zones that stretch for thousands of miles across the country.

Tundra, Taiga, Steppe, and Desert

While most of Russia is made up of plains, there are some spectacular mountain chains. The Caucasus Mountains, shown below, lie to the south of European Russia between the Black and Caspian seas.

In the far north is a zone of bleak, treeless plains known as tundra. Almost all of the tundra lies inside the Arctic Circle. Beneath a thin layer of vegetation is a permanent layer of ice, called permafrost (*see* p. 32). Most of the year, the tundra is covered with snow, but in summer it becomes a wetland of lakes and pools.

South of the tundra is a broad zone of marshy forests called taiga. Taiga covers more than half the country. Still farther south are the steppes—a zone of vast, treeless plains. The steppes are baking hot in summer and freezing cold in winter. On Russia's most southerly fringes, along the Caspian Sea, the landscape becomes desert.

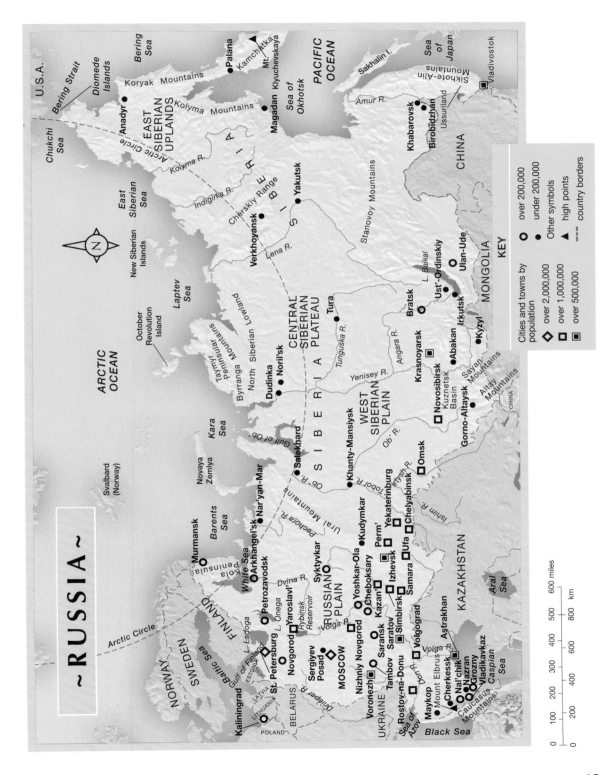

~RUSSIA~

KEY

Cities and towns by population
- over 2,000,000 ◇
- over 1,000,000 □
- over 500,000 ■
- over 200,000 ○
- under 200,000 ●

Other symbols
- ▲ high points
- - - - country borders

ARCTIC OCEAN

U.S.A.
Bering Strait
Diomede Islands
Bering Sea
Palana
Kamchatka
Mt. Klyuchevskaya
Koryak Mountains
Kolyma Mountains
Magadan
Sea of Okhotsk
PACIFIC OCEAN
Sakhalin I.
Sea of Japan
Sikhote-Alin Mountains
Vladivostok
Ussuriland
Khabarovsk
Birobidzhan
Amur R.
CHINA
MONGOLIA
Ulan-Ude
Ust'-Ordinskiy
Irkutsk
L. Baikal
Bratsk
Kyzyl
Abakan
Sayan Mountains
Altay Mountains
Gorno-Altaysk
Novosibirsk
Krasnoyarsk
Kuznetsk Basin
Omsk
Stanovoy Mountains
Angara R.
Yenisey R.
Tunguska R.
Tura
CENTRAL SIBERIAN PLATEAU
S I B E R I A
WEST SIBERIAN PLAIN
Khanty-Mansiysk
Ob' R.
Tobol R.
Irtysh R.
Ishim R.
Chelyabinsk
Yekaterinburg
Perm'
Ufa
KAZAKHSTAN
Aral Sea
Astrakhan
Caspian Sea

Anadyr
Chukchi Sea
Arctic Circle
EAST SIBERIAN UPLANDS
East Siberian Sea
Kolyma R.
Indigirka R.
Cherskiy Range
Verkhoyansk
Yakutsk
Lena R.
New Siberian Islands
Laptev Sea
October Revolution Island
Taymyr Peninsula
Byrranga Mountains
North Siberian Lowland
Dudinka
Noril'sk
Salekhard
Gulf of Ob'
Ob' R.
Ural Mountains
Pechora R.
Nar'yan-Mar
Kara Sea
Novaya Zemlya
Svalbard (Norway)
Barents Sea
Murmansk
Kola Peninsula
White Sea
Arkhangel'sk
Dvina R.
Onega
L. Onega
Petrozavodsk
L. Ladoga
Syktyvkar
Kudymkar
Yoshkar-Ola
Cheboksary
Kazan'
Izhevsk
Samara
Simbirsk
Saratov
Saransk
Tambov
Penza
Volgograd
Volga R.
Don R.
RUSSIAN PLAIN
Rybinsk Reservoir
Yaroslavl'
Sergiyev Posad
MOSCOW
Nizhniy Novgorod
Vladimir
Voronezh
Rostov-na-Donu
Sea of Azov
Maykop
Cherkessk
Nal'chik
Nazran
Grozny
Vladikavkaz
Mount Elbrus
Caucasus Mountains
Black Sea
UKRAINE
BELARUS
Dnieper R.
POLAND
LITHUANIA
LATVIA
ESTONIA
Kaliningrad
Baltic Sea
Gulf of Finland
St. Petersburg
Novgorod
FINLAND
SWEDEN
NORWAY
Arctic Circle

N

| 0 | 100 | 200 | 300 | 400 | 500 | 600 miles |
| 0 | 200 | 400 | 600 | 800 | km |

15

The Russian Plain: Russia's Heartland

Russia's vast landscape also changes from west to east, alternating between plains, mountains, and high plateaus. Great rivers run across the country, generally in a north–south or south–north direction. In the west of the country is the broad Russian Plain. This is the country's heartland. The plain is densely populated and home to four-fifths of Russia's population. It stretches from the borders of Ukraine, Belarus, Latvia, and Estonia east to the Ural Mountains, and from the shores of the Barents Sea south to the peaks of the Caucasus. Generally, the plain is quite flat, averaging only 560 feet (170 m) above sea level.

Some of Europe's greatest rivers flow across the Russian Plain, including the Volga (*see* box), Don, Dvina, and Dnieper. At some 1,160 miles (1,868 km), the Don is just under half the length of the Volga. Nevertheless, it is another important trading route, connecting the Russian heartlands with the Black Sea via the Sea of Azov.

The soils of the Russian Plain are generally poor and thin. Most of the northern part of the plain is covered by forests and dotted with lakes. This area supplies timber, furs, and fish. In the south, where soils are richer, farms produce wheat, rye, barley, sugar beet, sunflowers, and potatoes. Beef and dairy cattle are also raised here.

The southern part of the Russian Plain rises into the foothills of the Caucasus Mountains—in Russian,

The Volga

At 2,293 miles (3,689 km), the Volga is Europe's longest river. In ancient times, when the river was an important trade route used to bring amber from the Baltic Sea, the Greeks knew the Volga as the *Rha*. The Mongols called it the *Itil*.

The Volga rises in hills northwest of Moscow and snakes east then south across the Russian Plain, before emptying into the Caspian Sea at Astrakhan. Like many Russian rivers, the Volga has been dammed in several places to provide reservoirs for hydroelectric power stations. It remains a major water route, linked to the Don River by the Volga–Don Ship Canal, and to the Black Sea by the Volga–Baltic Waterway.

Along the Volga's banks are some of Russia's most important cities, including Volgograd and Kazan'. Because the river has played such an important role in Russian history, Russians call the river *Volga Mat'*—"Mother Volga."

Kavkaz. This range of jagged, snowcapped peaks stretches for 500 miles (800 km) between the Black and the Caspian seas, and reaches a height of 18,510 feet (5,642 m) at the summit of Mount Elbrus, the highest mountain in Europe. The Caucasus marks one of the traditional borders between Europe and Asia. Geologically, however, the mountains belong to Asia.

The Caucasus get their name from an ancient people who lived on the shores of the Black Sea— the Kaz-kaz.

The Urals: Between Europe and Asia

East of the Russian Plain lies another traditional border between Europe and Asia—the Ural Mountains. The Urals stretch north to south for 1,250 miles (2,000 km) from the border with Kazakhstan north to the shores of the Kara Sea. The mountains are mostly low and rounded in the south, but are steep and rocky in the north. This forested northern region is rich in minerals and timber.

Geographers often divide Russia both according to its landforms and its vegetation.

RUSSIA'S LAND AND TERRAIN

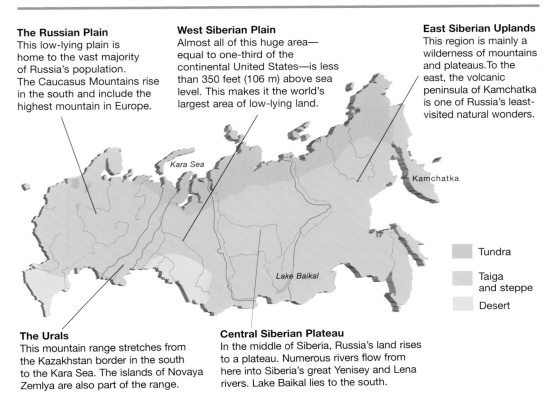

The Russian Plain
This low-lying plain is home to the vast majority of Russia's population. The Caucasus Mountains rise in the south and include the highest mountain in Europe.

West Siberian Plain
Almost all of this huge area— equal to one-third of the continental United States—is less than 350 feet (106 m) above sea level. This makes it the world's largest area of low-lying land.

East Siberian Uplands
This region is mainly a wilderness of mountains and plateaus. To the east, the volcanic peninsula of Kamchatka is one of Russia's least-visited natural wonders.

Kara Sea

Kamchatka

Lake Baikal

Tundra

Taiga and steppe

Desert

The Urals
This mountain range stretches from the Kazakhstan border in the south to the Kara Sea. The islands of Novaya Zemlya are also part of the range.

Central Siberian Plateau
In the middle of Siberia, Russia's land rises to a plateau. Numerous rivers flow from here into Siberia's great Yenisey and Lena rivers. Lake Baikal lies to the south.

Major deposits of petroleum and minerals have made the Urals an important area for mining, iron and steel production, and chemical industries. The desolate Arctic islands of Novaya Zemlya, north of the mainland, are also part of the Ural mountain range and were once used as a test site for nuclear bombs.

Siberia: "The Sleeping Land"

The vast region known as Siberia stretches east from the Urals to the Pacific and south from the Arctic Ocean to the borders of China, Mongolia, and Kazakhstan. Its name in Russian is *Sibir*, from a Mongolian (Tatar) word that means "sleeping land." The region is rich in natural resources, including timber, furs, hydroelectric power, and mineral deposits.

Geographers divide Siberia into three sections. East of the Urals is the immense West Siberian Plain. Most of the region is covered with a patchwork of forests, swamps, and lakes, merging into tundra in the far north. Two great rivers cross the plain—the Ob' and the Yenisey. The 2,540-mile-long (4,090 km) Yenisey River marks the plain's eastern edge.

Between the Yenisey and Lena rivers is another vast region—the Central Siberian Plateau. Here the land rises to between 1,000 and 2,300 feet (300–700 m) and is crisscrossed by numerous small rivers. In the south is Lake Baikal (*see* box opposite), the world's seventh-largest lake. Along the border with China and Mongolia are the high mountains of the Altay (*see* box) and Sayan ranges.

Between the Central Siberian Plateau and the Pacific Ocean is the third "chunk" of Siberia, a land of lofty mountains known as the East Siberian Uplands. Russia's Pacific coastline stretches a remarkable 10,000 miles (16,000 km), longer than any other

The Altay Mountains

The jagged Altay Mountains (*see* p. 28) first formed some 300 to 500 million years ago, during a period when many of the world's great mountains chains were made. The mountains' name means "golden" in Mongolian. They got their name owing to their appearance in the harsh desert sunlight. The mountains are also rich in mineral ores, especially copper, lead, and zinc. The great Ob' River has its source in the mountains.

Lake Baikal

Beautiful Lake Baikal, set deep in the heart of southern Siberia, holds 5,500 cubic miles (23,000 cu. km) of water—one-fifth of all the liquid freshwater in the world, and more than all of North America's Great Lakes combined.

Baikal is also the deepest lake in the world, with a bottom 5,314 feet (1,620 m) deep. In terms of surface area, it is 398 miles (636 km) long and covers some 12,200 square miles (31,500 sq. km), a greater area than the states of Maryland and Delaware added together.

The lake's clear, sparkling water supports around 2,000 species of plants and animals, three-quarters of which are found only in this lake. The wildlife ranges from sponges and water insects to the Baikal seal and includes many kinds of fish, such as the sturgeon (see p. 91).

country with shores on the Pacific. This coast is a wild region of mountains and islands, where the landscapes range from tundra in the north to thick forests in the south.

The Sikhote-Alin Mountains, stretching north from the port city of Vladivostok, are much warmer and wetter than the rest of Russia. The mountains are covered in thick, subtropical forest, an environment that has more in common with Southeast Asia than most of Russia.

The region includes the Kamchatka Peninsula and the beautiful Kuril Islands, which are the tips of a volcanic range of underwater mountains.

REPUBLICS AND PROVINCES

Many peoples live in the vast area of Russia, and this fact is reflected in the complicated political division of the country. Today, the Russian Federation includes not only the Russian Republic but 24 autonomous (self-ruling) republics, 1 autonomous province, or *oblast*, and 6 autonomous districts, or *okruga*. Many of these areas are small—for example, the collection of republics in the Caucasus. Some, however, are very large. The Sakha

REPUBLICS, PROVINCES, AND DISTRICTS OF RUSSIA

After the collapse of the Soviet Union, many areas of the Russian Republic declared their independence. In 1992, however, the central government in Moscow and the governments of these areas signed a treaty of federation and Russia officially became the Russian Federation. In 1993, a new constitution enshrined the rights of Russia's republics.

Russian Federal Republic
Autonomous republics
Autonomous districts
Autonomous province

AUTONOMOUS REPUBLICS
1 ADYGEA Maykop
2 KARACHAY-CHERKESSIA Cherkessk
3 KABARDINO-BALKARIA Nal'chik
4 NORTH OSSETIA (ALANIA) Vladikavkaz
5 INGUSHETIA Nazran
6 CHECHNYA Grozny
7 DAGESTAN Makhachkala
8 KALMYKIA Elista

9 KARELIA Petrozavodsk
10 MORDVINIA Saransk
11 CHUVASHIA Cheboksary
12 MARI EL Yoshkar-Ola
13 TATARSTAN Kazan'
14 UDMURTIA Izhevsk
15 BASHKORTOSTAN Ufa
16 KOMI Syktyvkar
17 YAMALIA Nar'yan-Mar
18 GORNO-ALTAY Gorno-Altaysk

19 KHAKASSIA Abakan
20 TUVA Kyzyl
21 BURYATIA Ulan-Ude
22 SAKHA Yakutsk
23 CHUKOTKA Anadyr
24 KORYAKIA Palana

AUTONOMOUS PROVINCE (OBLAST)
25 BIROBIJAN (YEVREY) Birobidzhan

AUTONOMOUS DISTRICTS (OKRUGA)
26 KHANTIA-MANSIA Khanty-Mansiyisk
27 TAYMYR IA Dudinka
28 UST'-ORDA Ust'Ordinskiy
29 AGA (AGINSKIY-BURYAT) Aginskoye
30 PERMYAKIA Kudymkar
31 EVENKIA Tura

Republic covers 1,198,146 square miles (3,103,198 sq. km)—almost twice the size of Alaska. The Russian Republic is itself divided into numerous *oblasti* and *krai*, or territories, which also have a measure of self-rule.

Many of these are the homelands of Russia's numerous native peoples but other ethnic groups will often live in these areas as well. Most, however, have large Russian populations, and although they are independent in name, they are controlled on the whole by Moscow.

European Russia

The heartlands of the sprawling Russian Republic are in western Russia and cover much of the Russian Plain. At the center of the plain is Moscow (*see* pp. 35–41), the capital of the Russian Republic as well as of the entire Russian Federation. Around the capital is a region of villages, woods, and farms, interrupted here and there by industrial development.

This Russian Orthodox cathedral, with its onion domes and whitewashed walls, is typical of many in European Russia.

Along the plain's great rivers are many old cities. The cathedrals and monasteries of cities such as Novgorod, Yaroslavl', and Sergiyev Posad have whitewashed walls and gold or silver onion domes that glint in the sunshine.

St. Petersburg (*see* p. 42–45), Russia's second-largest city, lies 400 miles (650 km) northwest of Moscow. North of St. Petersburg is the Republic of Karelia, which borders Finland. Much of its land is a wilderness of lake and forest. Two of its lakes—Ladoga and Onega—are the largest in Europe. The native inhabitants—the Karelians—are a Finno-Ugric people closely related to the Finns. The capital, which lies on the northern shores of Lake Ladoga, is Petrozavodsk.

North of Karelia is the Kola Peninsula, which is a part of the Russian Republic and which is separated from the rest of Russia's coast by the icy White Sea. The peninsula is covered by forest and tundra and is one of the traditional homelands of the Sami reindeer herders. The land is rich in mineral deposits, and thousands of acres of Sami lands are being polluted by sulfur poisoning from smelting factories built in the region.

On the Kola Peninsula's remote northern coast is the naval base and port of Murmansk. On the southeastern shore of the White Sea is Arkhangel'sk (known in English as Archangel)—the historic base of Russia's navy and an important trading center.

The Volga Region

As Stalingrad, Volgograd was the site of one of the turning-point battles of World War II. These massive sculptures of a Russian soldier and a sword-wielding Mother Russia commemorate the hundreds of thousands of Russians who died in the battle.

The importance of the Volga River for trade and settlements in southern European Russia is reflected by the area's name, the Volga Region. This part of the country is an important industrial center and a major grain-producing area. Cities on the Volga River include Nizhny Novgorod, where cars, ships, and MiG fighter aircraft are built; historic Kazan', capital

of the Tatar peoples since the 13th century and today capital of Tatarstan; Volgograd, which produces steel, aluminum, and machine parts; and Astrakhan, a trading port near the Caspian Sea.

Volgograd (Stalingrad) was the site of one of the most important battles of World War II (1939–1945), when the Soviet Army halted the advancing German forces. About one million Russians and 200,000 German soldiers were killed, and the city was reduced to rubble. The battle is commemorated by a huge statue—236 feet (72 m) high —of Mother Russia.

The Volga region has seven republics that serve as homelands for minority peoples. These include Tatarstan, a homeland for the Tatars, who for a long time resisted the growth of the Russian empire; and Kalmykia, which is home to the Kalmucks—Buddhist Mongolians who fled Mongolia in the 17th century.

Changing Names

Under Soviet rule, many of Russia's towns and cities were given new names that were more in keeping with the values of the communist regime. Cities whose names recalled the names of the country's czars, or emperors, were renamed after the heroes of the USSR. For example, Yekaterinburg—originally named for the czarina Catherine I and for St. Catherine—was renamed Sverdlovsk, after a local communist leader, Yakov Sverdlov. Similarly, St. Petersburg, or Petrograd ("Peter's Town"), and Volgograd were renamed Leningrad and Stalingrad in honor of two of the Soviet Union's greatest leaders, Lenin and Stalin. After the end of communist Russia in 1991, most cities whose names had been changed retook their old names.

Kaliningrad

On the shores of the Baltic Sea is Kaliningrad, a small wedge of Russian territory that is completely isolated from the rest of Russia. Kaliningrad is also the smallest province, or *oblast*, of the Russian Republic. Before World War II, the area belonged to Germany but was seized by the Soviet Union at the end of the war.

The city of Kaliningrad, once known by its German name, Königsberg, is a major naval base and fishing port. The surrounding region is famous as a source of amber, a fossilized pine resin used in making jewelry.

Kaliningrad is named after Mikhail Kalinin (1875–1946), Soviet head of state from 1919 to 1946.

Peoples and Republics of Caucasia

The imposing Caucasus Mountains and their foothills are home to a remarkable variety of peoples and languages. Seven of the Russian Federation's 22 republics are located in the Caucasus, and about 40 different languages are spoken by a population of only 13 million—all in an area about the size of Florida. Islam and Russian Orthodoxy are both widely practiced in the region. The area was at an ancient crossroads between Asia and Europe and was conquered by Russia only in the 19th century.

On the northern slopes of the Caucasus is a landscape with many hot mineral springs and dead volcanoes. This is Kavkazskie Mineralnye Vody (meaning "Caucasian mineral waters")—a popular vacation destination where visitors come to enjoy the natural bathing pools and mud baths. The warm and sunny coast of the nearby Black Sea is another popular vacation area.

One of the largest Caucasian republics is Dagestan, which has borders along the Caspian Sea. Its name translates into English as simply

Although the lowlands of the Caucasus region have a warmer climate than most parts of Russia, high in the mountains it is cold enough for glaciers to have formed.

"Mountain Kingdom," and its hot and dry landscape is home to some 81 nationalities. Most of Dagestan's population of two million are Muslim. Archaeologists claim that its inhabitants were one of the first peoples on Earth to plant crops and keep animals.

The people of Dagestan are very proud of their culture, and they are famous for their beautiful, intricately patterned carpets. Their national hero is Shāmil (about 1798–1871), who fought against the invading Russian armies in the 19th century, but was finally defeated and captured.

The neighboring republic of Chechnya is also strongly patriotic. Unlike Dagestan, however, the republic is openly hostile to Russian rule. During the 1990s, the Russians waged a fierce war with Chechen rebels fighting for the independence of their country (see p. 118).

The Ural Region

The city of Yekaterinburg ("Catherine's Town"), with a population of 1.4 million, is the capital of the Ural region. It was founded as a mining center in 1723 and grew rich during the 19th century when gold and platinum were discovered in nearby mountains. The city is also famous as the place where Czar Nicholas II and his wife and children were murdered in 1918, in the aftermath of the October Revolution.

During World War II, many arms factories were moved east of the Urals, out of reach of the advancing German armies. After the war, the region continued to produce much of Russia's military hardware, including nuclear weapons. In 1957, the city of Chelyabinsk suffered the world's worst nuclear accident before Chernobyl. Some nearby places still suffer from radioactive pollution.

Ethnic Tension

Since the breakup of the Soviet Union, much of Caucasia has been ravaged by war. Some of the worst fighting took place in 1992 in the republic of North Ossetia, where a minority of 500,000 Ingush lived among a majority of Ossetians. The Ingush minority wanted to join the neighboring Ingush homeland, the Ingushetia Republic. Tensions between the two peoples escalated into a bloody conflict, in which hundreds of people died. The Russian government in Moscow sent troops into North Ossetia to settle the dispute, but the Russian troops are said to have sided with the Ossetians. The whole Ingush minority fled to Ingushetia, and their property was confiscated or destroyed.

25

Settling Siberia

The Russians began to push their country's frontiers eastward in the 16th century, building towns and military forts as they went. The native peoples were unable to resist the onslaught of well-armed Russian soldiers. Four centuries later, under the Soviet Union, homelands were set up for the native peoples. These continue to exist under the Russian Federation, many of them as nominally independent republics. Today, large areas of Siberia remain part of the Russian Republic, providing it with a continuous corridor of land between west and east.

Throughout Russian history, Siberia has been notorious as a land of exile. Between 1650 and 1990, millions of criminals, religious dissenters, and political prisoners were exiled to Siberia. They were put to work in a network of remote labor camps, called Gulags (*see* p. 72) in Soviet times, where they toiled in mines, built highways and railroads, or worked in factories.

Today, most of Siberia's towns and cities are in the southern part of the region, along the lines of the Trans-Siberian and Baikal-Amur railroads (*see* p. 94). Major rivers such as the Lena and Yenisey are also important transportation routes. In summer, ships sail along the rivers; in winter, trucks drive over river water that is frozen solid to a depth of several feet. Many of the remote northern settlements can be reached only by air.

Novosibirsk (*see* pp. 46–47), the largest city in Siberia, lies at the southern edge of the West Siberian Plain. From Krasnoyarsk, river boats travel 1,250 miles (2,000 km) north along the Yenisey River to the Arctic port of Dudinka. The remote mining and

Villages and towns in Siberia are few and far between. Apart from a few major cities that were built to house migrant mine workers, settlements are small and ramshackle. The village of Listvyanka shown here lies on the western shores of Lake Baikal.

The Tunguska Event

At approximately 7:00 A.M. on June 30, 1908, a huge explosion ripped across the taiga of central Siberia, about 350 miles (560 km) north of Bratsk. The explosion was seen and heard up to 500 miles (800 km) away. Eyewitnesses reported earth tremors and a blast of hot wind. Tremors were picked up by earthquake detectors as far away as western Europe.

Because the region was remote and uninhabited, the site was not properly investigated until 1927. Scientists found that trees had been flattened in a radiating pattern up to 20 miles (32 km) from the epicenter of the explosion. An area of 800 square miles (2,070 sq. km) was devastated, and no plants were growing 20 years after the event. But there was no impact crater, suggesting that the explosion had taken place in the air.

It has been calculated that the Tunguska explosion was equivalent to the detonation of a 15 megaton bomb, 75 times the amount of energy that was released by the Hiroshima atomic bomb in 1945. Scientists now think that the Tunguska event was caused by a meteorite—perhaps 165 to 330 feet (50 to 100 m) in diameter—colliding with the Earth's atmosphere. Traveling at around 45,000 mph (72,400 kph), it generated so much heat that it vaporized in a huge aerial explosion about four to six miles (6 to 9 km) above the Earth's surface. Fortunately, this took place over an uninhabited area.

mineral processing city of Noril'sk exploits the huge deposits of copper, nickel, cobalt, and coal that are found in the north of the region.

Irkutsk is the administrative center for eastern Siberia. It is also a manufacturing and engineering town, using power supplied by a hydroelectric dam on the Angara River, which flows out of nearby Lake Baikal. On the eastern shore of the lake is the Barguzin National Reserve, Russia's oldest nature reserve, founded in 1917. The reserve contains 38 species of mammal, including the sable—a weasel-like creature—and the Baikal seal.

The city of Bratsk, 300 miles (480 km) to the north, has the largest aluminum smelting plant in the world, powered by one of the world's largest hydroelectric projects. Unfortunately, the plant and other local factories produce some of the worst pollution in Russia.

Taiga forests within about 60 miles (100 km) of Bratsk are dead or dying because of air pollution.

Two horsemen herd goats on the Altay Mountains in southern Siberia. Goats, along with sheep, cattle, yaks, and horses, are important to the livelihoods of the Altay people.

Siberian Peoples and Republics

Scattered around Siberia are the republics, provinces, and districts that serve as homelands for Russia's many native peoples. To the north are the homelands of the Nentsy, Dolgan, Evenki, Yakut, and Khanty peoples.

The vast Sakha Republic (formerly Yakutia) is a land of swampy forest. The Yakut people, who make up about a third of the republic's population, are brilliant craftspeople and have a lively literature. Like many of the peoples of northern Siberia, they are shamanists (*see* p. 114).

In the 19th century, gold was discovered along the Lena River in Yakutia. The region quickly became a Russian version of America's "Wild West." The Sakha capital, Yakutsk, was once a frontier town inhabited by gold-miners. Today, however, it is better known as one of the few cities in the world to be built entirely on permafrost (*see* p. 32).

In the south, along the Mongolian and Chinese borders, are four republics—Gorno-Altay, Khakassia, Tuva, and Buryatia. The mountainous Gorno-Altay

Republic is home to the native Altay—a Turkic-speaking people. There are wild rivers, spectacular waterfalls, and awesome glaciers in Altay, as well as steppe and taiga. The area was once home to the Pazyryk people, who buried the mummified bodies of their chieftains together with chariots, carpets, and carvings.

The remote republic of Tuva is home to the semi-nomadic Tuvans, who follow a Mongolian culture and the Tibetan Buddhist religion. Tuva is a land of rolling hills and forests, steppe and desert. The land supports herds of camels, cows, and reindeer. For a long time, the area was ruled by China but became part of Russia at the beginning of the 20th century.

Territories of the Russian Far East

The Russian Far East encompasses all the Russian territories (*krai*) that border the Pacific Ocean. In addition, in the far northeast, are the remote, bleak homelands of the Chukchi and Koryak peoples—Chukotka and Koryakia. To the south of Koryakia stretches the Kamchatka Peninsula, the "land of ice and fire" (*see* p. 30). Its most important city is the naval base of Petropavlovsk.

In the far south is Primorsky Kray ("Maritime Territory")—an arm of land sandwiched between the Sea of Japan and China. The territory is dominated by the port city of Vladivostok (*see* pp. 46–47), which is at the end of the Trans-Siberian Railway.

North of Vladivostok is Ussuriland, home to the most northerly monsoon forests in the world. The forests flood in summer, but are often dry in winter. Vines and lianas (tropical climbing plants) twist around the tree trunks, and the forest floor is smothered with undergrowth. Off the coast is the island of Sakhalin (*see* box).

Sakhalin

The fish-shaped, rugged Sakhalin Island looks like a continuation of the string of islands that make up Japan to the south. The surrounding waters teem with fish and seals, and the inland parts of the island are made up of mountains and bamboo-covered plains. Before the 19th century, Sakhalin was settled by the Ainu, a native people of Japan. In the 19th century, Russia seized the island and turned it into a penal colony. Russian playwright Anton Chekhov, who visited the colony, wrote: "I have seen Ceylon, which is paradise, and Sakhalin, which is hell." Today, the island prospers on its rich fish stocks, and the Japanese and Russians work together to extract the island's oil.

Kamchatka: Land of Ice and Fire

Kamchatka has one of the most unstable terrains on Earth. Deep below the surface of the landscape, powerful natural forces are at work. The peninsula has more than 250 volcanoes, 70 of which are active. The highest volcano, at 15,585 feet (4,750 m), is Mount Klyuchevskaya, which last erupted in 1994. The volcanoes are surrounded by lava fields, creating a pocked, moonlike landscape.

Volcanoes are not the only sign of the underground activity. The landscape is dotted with hot springs, rivers, and spectacular geysers—natural jets of piping-hot water.

In Kronotsky National Park (left), some 200 geysers spurt mud, steam, and water high into the sky. Here a geyser lies temporarily dormant, while clouds of steam rise from erupting geysers in the background.

Until 1990, very few people were able to visit the spectacular landscapes of the Kamchatka Peninsula. This was not only because of the province's remoteness but because during the Cold War (*see* pp. 74–77), it was an important military site. Today, however, people are free to visit this beautiful and awesome "land of ice and fire."

CLIMATE

Russia's climate is shaped by the country's northern location and huge size. In general, Russian winters are long, cold, and dark, and the summers short and warm.

Land of Snow and Darkness

In Moscow, the first snow may fall at the end of October and not melt finally until mid-March. The Moskva River, which flows through the capital, freezes over in mid-November and does not thaw until April. Whenever people go out, they are sure to wrap themselves in furs and wear fur hats to keep warm. In Russia's Arctic ports, such as Murmansk and Arkhangel'sk, ships called ice-breakers have to work hard to keep harbors free of ice.

In Murmansk—the world's northernmost city—the sun does not set between May and July. These light-filled "nights" are called "white nights." Between November and January, the polar nights north of the Arctic Circle are very long. These effects are due to the tilt of the Earth's axis, which causes the North and South poles to face toward the sun alternately in summer and winter.

Russia's freezing winter fails to deter this hardy woman from taking a dip in a St. Petersburg park.

Being farther from the moderating effect of the sea, the Siberian city of Irkutsk experiences more extreme winter temperatures than Moscow.

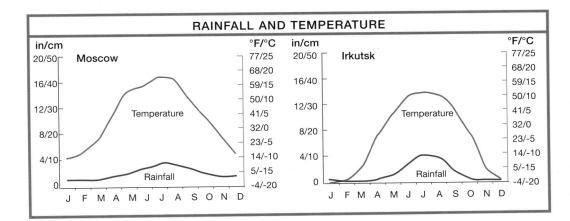

RAINFALL AND TEMPERATURE

Moscow

in/cm: 20/50, 16/40, 12/30, 8/20, 4/10, 0

°F/°C: 77/25, 68/20, 59/15, 50/10, 41/5, 32/0, 23/-5, 14/-10, 5/-15, -4/-20

Temperature

Rainfall

J F M A M J J A S O N D

Irkutsk

in/cm: 20/50, 16/40, 12/30, 8/20, 4/10, 0

°F/°C: 77/25, 68/20, 59/15, 50/10, 41/5, 32/0, 23/-5, 14/-10, 5/-15, -4/-20

Temperature

Rainfall

J F M A M J J A S O N D

From West to East

Warm, moist air from the Atlantic Ocean's Gulf Stream moderates the climate of European Russia, preventing extremes of heat and cold. This effect decreases the farther one goes away from the sea, and a so-called "continental" climate develops. This is marked by extremes of temperature—hot in summer and very cold in winter—and low rainfall. Central and eastern Siberia, for example, have temperatures ranging from 65°F (18°C) in the summer to -50°F (-45°C) in the winter.

The climate of the southern steppe, which borders on the desert plains of Kazakhstan, is drier and warmer than the central Russian Plain. In contrast, southern areas of the Russian Far East have a northern monsoon climate with warm, wet summers and cold, dry winters.

Permafrost

Permafrost is ground that is permanently frozen because the average annual air temperature is 32°F (0°C) or lower. This is the temperature that water freezes at. All the moisture in the soil and the fractured rocks beneath the surface is frozen to a thickness that varies from a few hundred to several thousand feet. In northern Siberia, the permafrost is about 5,000 feet (1,525 m) thick.

More than half the territory of Russia is permafrost. This causes many problems for mining and construction engineers. Anything built on permafrost begins to thaw out the frozen ground below. The ground becomes soft and muddy, and the roads or buildings begin to sink (subside). In the Siberian city of Yakutsk, the Russian Academy of Sciences founded an Institute of Permafrost to study the science of building on frozen ground. Experiments showed that to avoid problems with subsidence, buildings had to be supported on insulated piles bored at least 33 feet (10 m) into the permafrost. Yakutsk, the capital of the Sakha Republic, is one of the few cities in the world to be built on permafrost.

One of the most fascinating aspects of permafrost is how it can preserve dead animals and plants. The bodies of woolly mammoths, which roamed the Siberian plains 10,000 years ago but are now extinct, have been found almost perfectly preserved in the icy grip of the permafrost. One of these mammoths, discovered in 1902, is displayed in the Museum of Zoology in St. Petersburg.

ANIMALS AND PLANTS

The vegetation and wildlife of Russia are closely related to the three broad landscape zones that stretch west to east across the country—tundra, taiga, and steppe (*see* p. 14). The cold and largely treeless tundra supports a small number of animal species that are well adapted to the harsh conditions of their environment.

Herds of reindeer roam northward in the summer, feeding on the mosses and lichens that thinly cover the ground. Lemmings—small rodents that burrow under the snow in winter—provide a source of food for the snowy owl and the Arctic fox. The latter is particularly well adapted to the bitter climate, with fur on the underside of its paws and a coat that changes from grayish brown to snow-white in winter. Huge flocks of geese, ducks, and swans fly north to nest in the tundra during its brief summer.

Reindeer, along with cattle and sheep, are reared in Siberia despite the inhospitable climate. Here reindeer are herded in the republic of Chukotka, in northeast Siberia.

Animals of the Taiga and Steppe

In the forest-covered taiga to the south, larch is the dominant kind of tree east of the Urals. Unlike other conifers (cone-bearing trees), the larch drops its needles in winter, which helps it shed the heavy snowfalls.

Among the wildlife of the taiga is the sable, a member of the weasel family. Russian trappers have long hunted the sable for its fine fur, which is made into coats and hats.

The Siberian Tiger

The Siberian tiger (*Panthera tigris altaica*) is one of the world's rarest animals. Larger than the tigers of India and Southeast Asia, it has longer fur and is a paler yellow in color. Some Siberian tigers are up to 10 feet (3.15 m) long and may weigh up to 800 pounds (360 kg).

By 1948, when it was declared a protected species, the Siberian tiger had been hunted almost to extinction. Since then, its numbers have increased from around 20 or 30 to around 400, of which approximately 250 live along the Amur River in the Russian Far East. The tigers eat whatever they can catch, mostly wild boar, but also sika deer and young elk.

Brown bears are common in the forests and mountains throughout the country, from Europe to the Pacific coast. Siberian brown bears are larger than average, weighing up to 800 pounds (360 kg)—almost as big as the grizzly.

In the northerly areas of the steppe, deer, wild boar, and mink roam among the woods of birch, spruce, oak, and ash. Farther south, the steppe woodlands give way to a vast plain that is similar to the American prairie. With its rich black soil called *chernozem*, most of the steppe has been converted to farmland. However, antelopes, squirrels, and many birds make their home there.

Endangered Species

Russia's environmental problems (*see* p. 86) have taken their toll on the country's wildlife. The World Conservation Union's Red List includes big cats such as the Siberian tiger (*see* box) and Amur leopard; sea mammals such as the gray seal and several species of whale; the bison; birds such as the Siberian crane and Blakiston's fish owl; the Caucasian viper; and nine species of sturgeon.

RUSSIA'S CITIES

Almost three-quarters of the Russian population live in towns and cities. Many new cities were built during the Soviet period as part of a massive program of industrialization, and millions of people moved from the countryside to work in the new factories.

Moscow: The Russian Capital

Moscow—in Russian, *Moskva*—is the capital of Russia. The city is the cultural and industrial center of the country. With a population of nine million, Moscow is the country's biggest city by far, twice the size of St. Petersburg, the next-largest city, and ten times the size of Russia's other major cities. People from Moscow are called Muscovites.

> **Russia's chief cities are Moscow, St. Petersburg, Nizhniy Novgorod, Novosibirsk, Yekaterinburg, Samara, Omsk, Chelyabinsk, Kazan', Ufa, and Rostov.**

METROPOLITAN MOSCOW

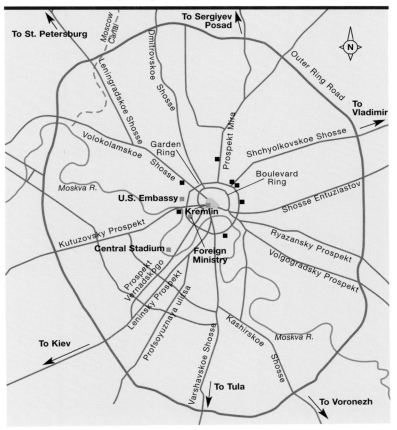

Metropolitan Moscow (the city center and its surrounding suburbs) is circled by four ring roads. The inner ring, which lies just to the north of the Kremlin, can be seen on the downtown Moscow map (see p. 37). The outer ring road lies some 9 to 12 miles (15–19 km) from the Kremlin. In between are the Boulevard and Garden ring roads. Avenues (prospekty) and highways (shosse) radiate from the center.

■ Train stations
▪ Downtown area

Sergiyev Posad

Forty-five miles (72 km) to the northeast of Moscow is the town of Sergiyev Posad. At the heart of the town is the ancient monastery of St. Sergius (1321–1391), who is Russia's patron saint. The monastery has two beautiful cathedrals, home to some of Russia's greatest art treasures. The Cathedral of the Assumption (below) is famous for its star-spangled domes and as the burial place of Czar Boris Godunov. In Soviet Russia, the monastery was for a while the seat of the Russian patriarch, leader of the Russian Orthodox church. Today, it remains one of Russia's most important spiritual centers.

The capital lies deep in the heart of the Russian Plain, in the broad, shallow valley of the Moskva (Moscow) River, a tributary of the Volga. It has a continental climate, with short, hot summers and long, cold, dark winters. The first frosts arrive in October, and snow stays on the ground until mid-March.

Getting around downtown is best done by walking, but for traveling longer distances, Moscow has a good network of buses and trams. Moscow also has one of the biggest and best subway systems in the world—the Moscow Metro (*see* pp. 38–39). Passenger boats and hydrofoils travel up and down the Moskva River in summer (it is iced over in winter). It is even possible to take a ship from Moscow to St. Petersburg in the north or Astrakhan in the south.

The city is laid out like a wheel, with highways extending like spokes from the center. These highways are interlinked by circular ring roads. At the hub of the wheel lies the Kremlin ("fortress"), the seat of Russian power for more than 900 years.

This center of Russian power sits on a hilltop on the north bank of the Moskva River and has been fortified since the early 12th century. The castle walls and bristling towers of today's Kremlin were built between 1475 and 1516 during the reign of the Russian czar Ivan the

DOWNTOWN MOSCOW

Bolshoi Theater

Senate Building

OKHOTNY RYAD

TEATRALNY PROEZD

LUBYANSKY PROEZD

TVERSKAYA ULITSA

Memorial to the Victims of Totalitarianism

NIKOLSKAYA ULITSA

VOZDVIZHENKA ULITSA

Moscow State University

MANEZH SQUARE

State History Museum

GUM Building

BOGOYAVLENSKY RYBNY PEREULOK

ULITSA LLINKA

N

Alexandrovsky Garden

Arsenal

RED SQUARE

Senate

Lenin Mausoleum

KHRUSTALNY

KITAYGORODSKY PROEZD

ULITSA VOZDVIZHENKA

MOKHOVAYA ULITSA

MANEZHNAYA ULITSA

Russian State Library

KREMLIN

Assumption Cathedral

Archangel Cathedral

St. Basil's Cathedral

Central Concert Hall

MOSKVORETSKAYA NABEREZHNAYA

Moskva River

KREMLYOVSKAYA NABEREZHNAYA

Great (*see* p. 55). The buildings within the walls date from the 15th century to the 1960s. The 18th-century Senate building, with its yellow ocher walls and large, green dome, houses the offices of the Russian president.

The oldest buildings in the Kremlin, though, are the churches. These are crowned with golden domes, topped with gilded crosses, which rise above the red-brick ramparts. The Kremlin is not only the center of political power. It was also once the center of the Russian Orthodox church. Archangel Cathedral contains the tombs of all Russia's rulers—except Boris Godunov—from the 1320s to 1682.

To the northeast of the Kremlin lies Red Square, famous in the past as the site of Soviet military parades. The square is dominated by the multicolored spires and onion domes of St. Basil's Cathedral (*see* p. 6), built in 1555–1561. St. Basil's is probably the most famous tourist sight in Russia.

*Moscow's city center lies in the shadow of the Kremlin, the seat of Russia's rulers for hundreds of years. In the center are broad streets (*ulitsi*) and passages (*proezdi*) as well as spacious squares (*ploshchadi*).*

Москва

This is how the Russian word for "Moscow"— Moskva—is spelled in the Cyrillic alphabet.

The Moscow Metro

There are not many cities in the world where an underground railway system counts as a tourist attraction. Moscow's subway, known as the *Metro*, is not just an extraordinary piece of transportation engineering; many of its stations are marvels of monumental art.

Construction of the Metro began in 1932 under the direction of Joseph Stalin—dictator of the Soviet Union from 1924 to 1953—and the system is still being expanded today. There are eight lines running out from the downtown area. These are interconnected by one circular line. The entire metro has a total of 125 miles (200 km) of track and 150 stations. Trains run every three minutes—once a minute during rush hours.

The stations and tunnels were built very deep underground, so that the stations could double as air-raid shelters. In the first six months of World War II (1939–1945), the Metro provided a shelter for more than 15 million people. Government officials set up movie projectors on the platforms and screened propaganda films for their captive audiences.

The stations built between 1932 and 1954 are richly decorated with intricate mosaics, frescoes, monuments, stained glass, chandeliers, and sculptures. Only the finest materials were used—bronze, stainless steel, rare woods, gilt, crystal, and 23 different kinds of polished marble. Each station is designed differently and has a theme that glorifies some aspect of the Soviet Union—the October Revolution, Russian military power, industrial achievements, agriculture, or a region of the former USSR, such as Ukraine. The design for one of the finest stations—Mayakovskaya—won the grand prize at the 1939 New York World's Fair. Other stations of note are Komsomolskaya (shown opposite),

which has mosaics of famous generals and soldiers from Russian history, and Ploshchad Revolyutsii, where sculptures portray the ideals of socialism.

Stations are marked outside with an "M" sign, and a ride costs around 10 cents. People who try to avoid paying are stopped by metal arms that come out from automatic entry gates. The Metro is the easiest and quickest way to get around the city, and it carries 3.1 billion passengers each year—more than any other subway system in the world.

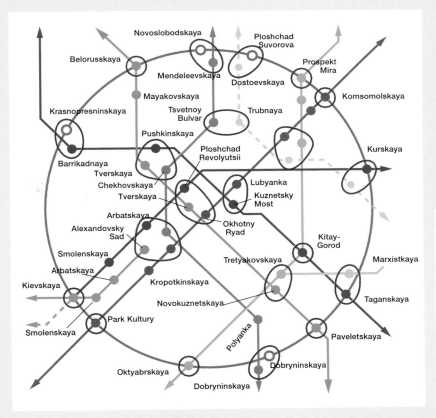

This map shows only the central area of the Moscow Metro, inside the Koltsevaya (Circle) Line. Dotted lines show Metro lines that are under construction.

Sokolnicheskaya Line
Zamoskvoretskaya Line
Arbatsko-Pokrovskaya Line
Filyovskaya Line
Koltsevaya (Circle) Line
Kaluzhsko-Rizhskaya Line
Tagansko-Krasno-presninskaya Line
Kalininskaya Line
Serpukhovsko-Timiryazevskaya Line
Lines under construction

The Lenin Mausoleum

After Lenin's death in 1924, Russia's communist leaders decided that Lenin's body was too precious to be buried and determined to display it instead in a specially built tomb, or mausoleum. Chemists worked in a gloomy cellar beneath Red Square to develop a secret new embalming fluid that, they hoped, would preserve the corpse forever. Finally, in the summer of 1924, the body was ready for display, and the mausoleum became a site of pilgrimage for millions of Russians. Lenin's body has lain in the mausoleum ever since, except for a period during World War II, when it was taken to Siberia for safety. From 1953 to 1961, Stalin's embalmed body lay in the mausoleum beside Lenin.

On the west side of the square is the Lenin Mausoleum (*see* box). Here the embalmed body of Lenin, founder of the Soviet Union, lies preserved in a glass case. Behind the mausoleum, in a special plot beneath the Kremlin wall, other famous people are buried, including Joseph Stalin and the Russian astronaut Yuri Gagarin.

The spectacular GUM building—the *Gosudarstvenny Universalniy Magazin*, or State Department Store—was once filled with bare shelves and long lines of waiting people. Today, it is a glittering shopping mall with designer boutiques. The large Manezh Square, once a holding area for the huge military parades through neighboring Red Square, is now a pedestrian area complete with an underground shopping mall.

Russia's largest department store, GUM, was built in the 19th century and housed over 1,000 shops. Since the end of the Soviet Union, the GUM has been transformed by privatization into a busy and efficient shopping mall full of designer stores.

The downtown area around the Kremlin is a mixture of colorful historic buildings and drab office and apartment buildings. Moscow has changed beyond recognition since the end of the Soviet period. Western businesses have moved in, and American fast-food pizza and hamburger restaurants have appeared beneath billboards advertising American cigarettes.

Russia's rich cultural heritage is preserved in the capital's many museums. The best of pre-Revolutionary Russian art is displayed in the Tretyakov Gallery, across the Moskva River to the south of the Kremlin. There are many beautiful old icons (religious paintings on wooden panels), as well as masterpieces by more modern artists.

Nearby is the entrance to Gorky Park, where Muscovites stroll among ponds and flower gardens beside the river and enjoy the rides and roller coasters in the amusement park. In winter, the ponds freeze over to make giant open-air ice rinks.

Visitors to Moscow's Gorky Park can take part in many activities, including boating and tennis. The park, though, is particularly magical in winter, when it fills with skaters and children playing in the snow. Opened in 1925, the park is named for the Soviet writer Maxim Gorky (1868–1936).

The eastern end of Vasilevsky Island is known as the Strelka, or "Tongue of Land." The Strelka became the center of Russia's sea trade, and today is home to the Stock Exchange as well as many museums. Visible here are the Zoological (left), Naval (center), and Agricultural (right) museums. Across the river is the spire of the Admiralty building.

St. Petersburg: "The Venice of the North"

St. Petersburg is Russia's second-largest city, with a population of about 4,500,000. It lies 400 miles (640 km) northwest of Moscow. It was founded by Czar Peter the Great in 1703 and was the capital of Russia from 1712 to 1918. It was here that the Russian czars lived and ruled for 200 years, until they were overthrown in the October Revolution (*see* pp. 66–67).

The city was built on the marshy banks of the Neva River, at the eastern end of the Gulf of Finland. To drain the land, numerous canals had to be built, earning St. Petersburg the nickname "the Venice of the North." The city was built in imitation of western European cities, with elegant palaces and public buildings laid out along the broad embankments and boulevards. St. Petersburg, with its access to the Baltic Sea, is also an important seaport and naval base.

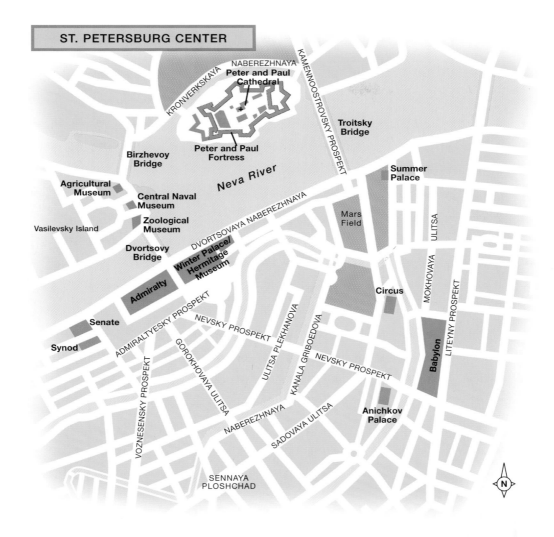

ST. PETERSBURG CENTER

KRONVERKSKAYA

NABEREZHNAYA

Peter and Paul Cathedral

KAMENNOOSTROVSKY PROSPEKT

Peter and Paul Fortress

Troitsky Bridge

Birzhevoy Bridge

Agricultural Museum

Central Naval Museum

Summer Palace

Neva River

Zoological Museum

Vasilevsky Island

Dvortsovy Bridge

DVORTSOVAYA NABEREZHNAYA

Mars Field

ULITSA

Winter Palace/ Hermitage Museum

MOKHOVAYA

Admiralty

Circus

LITEYNY PROSPEKT

Senate

ADMIRALTYESKY PROSPEKT

NEVSKY PROSPEKT

Synod

GOROKHOVAYA ULITSA

ULITSA PLEKHANOVA

KANALA GRIBOEDOVA

NEVSKY PROSPEKT

Babylon

VOZNESENSKY PROSPEKT

NABEREZHNAYA

SADOVAYA ULITSA

Anichkov Palace

SENNAYA PLOSHCHAD

N

At the heart of the city is the Peter and Paul Fortress located on the north bank of the river. Between 1703 and 1917, many political prisoners were locked up in the dungeons of the fortress, including writers Fyodor Dostoyevsky and Maxim Gorky and even Peter the Great's own son Alexey.

The Cathedral of Saints Peter and Paul, in the middle of the fort, is a well-known city landmark, with a slender, needlelike spire that stands 400 feet (122 m) high. Inside the cathedral are the tombs of Peter the Great and his successors, including the members of the Romanov

Like Venice, St. Petersburg is a city that seems to float on water. The broad Neva River snakes through the city, and numerous canals flow among the impressive buildings and grand avenues (prospekty).

"Hero City"

St. Petersburg had three different names in the 20th century. As St. Petersburg, the city was the Russian capital at the outbreak of World War I in 1914, when Russia went to war with Germany. In an anti-German reaction, the city's name was changed to the more Russian-sounding Petrograd. Both names mean "Peter's City."

In 1924, the name was changed again to Leningrad, in honor of the revolutionary leader, Vladimir Ilyich Lenin. As Leningrad, it was later awarded the status of "hero city." This was because of the terrible suffering the inhabitants underwent during World War II. In September 1941, the German army set up a blockade around the city. The only way to send in food was by truck across frozen Lake Ladoga to the east of the city. By the end of the siege, in January 1943, 670,000 people had died of hunger and illness.

After the breakup of the Soviet Union, in 1991, the people voted to change the name of the city back to St. Petersburg.

The Winter Palace has been the site of some of the most important events in Russia's history (see p. 64)

royal family who were murdered by the communists in Yekaterinburg in 1918 (*see* p. 68).

Across the Neva River is the Winter Palace, with its beautiful facade. The palace was built for Catherine the Great in the mid-18th century. Once the home of the Russian royal family, it now houses part of the Hermitage Museum, one of the biggest and

best art collections in the world. Someone has calculated that if a visitor were to spend just ten seconds looking at each item on display, it would take three and a half years to see everything in the museum.

One of the city's most famous streets is Nevsky Prospekt. Built during the reign of Peter the Great, Nevsky Prospekt leads from the Alexander Nevsky Monastery—named after a prince of Rus' who won a great triumph over the Swedes in 1240 (*see* p. 54)—toward the Neva River.

Nevsky Prospekt is a broad avenue 2.8 miles (4.5 km) long. During the day, the street is crowded with shoppers and tourists, and there are five Metro stations along its length. Many important buildings are found on the avenue, including Kazan' Cathedral, the Pushkin Theater, and several palaces.

St. Petersburg's main thoroughfare is Nevsky Prospekt. This busy avenue stretches southeast from the Admiralty building, whose gleaming golden spire is seen here in the background.

NOVOSIBIRSK

Circus

Cathedral of the Ascension

ULITSA GOGOLYA

Central Market

ULITSA NARYMSKAYA

ULITSA SOVIETSKAYA

ULITSA KRYLOVA

ULITSA DERZHAVINA

Stadium

ULITSA FRUNZE

ULITSA ROMANOVA

Central Park

ULITSA POTANINSKAYA

VOKZALNAYA MAGISTRAL

ULITSA YADRINTSYOVSKAYA

N

ULITSA ORDZHONIKIDZE

ULITSA LENINA

PLOSHCHAD LENINA

Opera and Ballet Theater

The focus of Novosibirsk is Lenin Square (Ploshchad Lenina), the site of the city's famous Opera House.

Novosibirsk: "New Siberia"

Novosibirsk, with a population of 1.5 million, is famous as the biggest city in Siberia. It lies in the middle of a vast plain, about 1,800 miles (2,880 km) east of Moscow. With its drab sprawl of smoky factories and concrete apartment buildings, Novosibirsk is typical of many cities built during the Soviet period.

The city was founded in 1893 where the Trans-Siberian Railway crosses the broad Ob' River. During the 1920s and 1930s, it rapidly developed as an industrial center and transportation hub for shipping the rich mineral deposits of Siberia to western Russia. Originally called Novonikolaevsk, after the last Russian czar, Nicholas II, Novosibirsk's Soviet name means "New Siberia."

The inhabitants of Novosibirsk are very proud of their city. The city downtown, based around Lenin Square, is dominated by the huge silver dome of the Opera House, Russia's biggest theater. Because of the famous dance and opera companies that perform there, it is known as "Siberia's Bolshoi." One of Russia's best ballet schools is also located at the theater.

There are also an art gallery, several museums, and botanic gardens in the city center. There are two handsome cathedrals and a small chapel, which is said to stand at the geographic center of Russia. Public transportation in Novosibirsk is provided by buses and trolleybuses and a single-line subway.

The people of Novosibirsk like to stroll in the handsome Central Park. With its horse-drawn carts and children's railway, there is lots to do. On cold Siberian days, many people may pay a visit to the steamy public bathhouses. On summer weekends, they may make boat trips on the Ob' or drive out to the Obskoe More—the "Ob' Sea." There they can swim or take walks in the beautiful, peaceful woods that edge the reservoir's shore.

On the southern outskirts of Novosibirsk, close to the Obskoe More, lies Akademgorodok ("Academic Town"). The town was built in the 1950s as a scientific research center, with homes for more than 65,000 workers and their families. Today, the town houses the well-regarded Novosibirsk State University, more than 20 scientific research institutes, and several museums.

These drab and uniform apartment buildings in the suburbs of Novosibirsk are typical of many towns and cities built during the Soviet period.

Vladivostok: "Lord of the East"

Vladivostok is located on a hilly peninsula above Golden Horn Bay on Russia's Pacific Coast. The city is certainly remote—a nine-hour flight from Moscow—and its name means "Lord of the East." For many years, few people knew anything about Vladivostok. As the main naval base for the Soviet Pacific Fleet, it was closed to all foreigners from 1958 to 1990. It is the capital of Primorsky Krai ("Maritime Territory") and has a population of almost 700,000.

For more than a hundred years, Vladivostok's harbor has been the base for Russia's Pacific Fleet. Today, however, container ships and ferries are more likely to be found moored at the docks.

The city was founded in 1860 as a military outpost, but its fine natural harbor was soon put to use as a commercial port and a base for the Russian Pacific Fleet. In 1891, it became the final stop for the Trans-Siberian Railway, and it is now the biggest and most important city in the Russian Far East.

The focus of the downtown is a large, busy square overlooking the Golden Horn Bay. People gather in the square to listen to local bands or to listen to political speeches. On the western side of the square is the White House, the seat of the local administration.

Nearby, overlooking the harbor on the Ulitsa Korabelnaya Naberezhnaya, are reminders of the city's naval history. A "Red Banner" submarine has been moored permanently on the grass and today serves as a museum. During World War II, the submarine sank ten enemy ships. Floating in the harbor is *Krasny Vimpel* ("Red Pennant"), the Pacific Fleet's first ship, which has also been converted into a museum. The city's history is celebrated as well in the Museum of the Pacific Fleet, which is housed in a former church.

Today, the city is no longer the great naval port it once was. Many ships from the Pacific Fleet have been abandoned and lie rusting in the docks. Local people want to use Vladivostok's location in the Far East, close to lucrative markets in Japan and Korea, as a way of rebuilding their city as an important business and trading center.

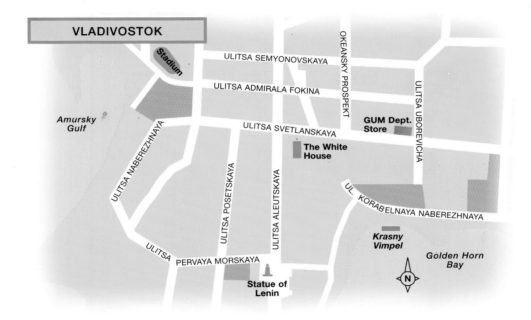

Vladivostok is situated among some of Russia's wildest landscapes. Local people often take a ferry out to one of the numerous islands that lie to the south of the city. Some people are lucky enough to own a dacha (cottage) there. Other ferries carry daytrippers across the Amursky Gulf to the port of Slavyanka, where there are plenty of sunny beaches, although the water can be cold. However, few people visit, or are able to visit, the island of Russky, which is owned by the Pacific Fleet. The island is shrouded in secrecy and is said to be home to an arsenal.

Vladivostok's downtown has traditionally been focused on the avenues close to its harbor.

Past and Present

"I cannot forecast to you the action of Russia. It is a riddle wrapped in a mystery inside an enigma."

British prime minister Winston Churchill in a broadcast speech, 1939

Over the centuries, the territory that today makes up the Russian Federation has been home to many peoples—Scythians, Sarmatians, and Slavs, to name but a few. The history of Russia itself, though, begins with a confederation of Slavic principalities called Rus', ruled by a dynasty of Vikings from Scandinavia.

Medieval Russia was confined to the fertile plains around the Volga and Dvina rivers. Beginning in the 16th century, however, the country's rulers, or *czars*, built a powerful empire that stretched across the Asian continent. Many peoples were conquered, and many ethnic Russians went to live in new settlements that were sometimes thousands of miles from the Russian capital, Moscow.

The Russian empire depended on the virtual enslavement of millions of peasants, called serfs. During the 19th century, as Russia industrialized, people grew restless, and there were calls for change. In 1917, a revolution overthrew the czar and replaced the empire with the world's first communist country—the Soviet Union.

The Communist Party wrought massive changes in Russia, creating a political and economic superpower that rivaled the United States. The cost of the Soviet Union's achievements was high: the denial of its citizens' freedom and other human rights. In 1991, another—democratic—revolution swept away the communist regime, and Russia entered another period of change and uncertainty.

This wood-panel painting, or icon, shows Saint Cyril, who, with his brother, Saint Methodius, first converted many of the Slavic peoples to Christianity.

FACT FILE

- In this book, the names of Russia's czars and other important historical figures are spelled in English—for example, Catherine rather than the Russian *Yekaterina*.

- The wife of a Russian czar was called a *czarina*. A son of a czar was called a *czarevich*, and a daughter, *czarevna*.

- The U.S. state of Alaska once belonged to Russia. The United States bought the territory from Russia in 1867 for $7.2 million.

- It is estimated that about 8.5 million Soviet citizens were put in prison, exiled, or executed during the Great Terror of the late 1930s.

EARLY TIMES

In ancient times, what is today southern Russia was home to nomadic (wandering) peoples, who herded sheep and cattle. The ancient Greek historian Herodotus (about 484–420 B.C.) wrote about a fierce people called the Scythians who lived on the steppes north of the Black Sea. They were expert horsemen and mighty warriors and they buried their chiefs, together with their horses and grooms, in underground tombs.

Sarmatians, Khazars, and Slavs

At the end of the fourth century B.C., another nomadic people, the Sarmatians, migrated to the Black Sea steppes from Central Asia and gradually forced the Scythians from their homelands. The Sarmatians ruled the area for about eight centuries, before they, too, were replaced by a succession of other peoples, including the Huns, Goths, and Khazars. The Khazars built a capital, called Itil, close to the mouth of the Volga River.

The Scythians excelled as artists and craftspeople. This gold figure of a Scythian warrior on horseback and armed with a spear dates back to the fourth century B.C. It was found at Kul Oba, a site in the Crimea.

The Russians themselves, though, are descended from a people called the East Slavs. Originally from Asia, the Slavs gradually migrated westward, settling across much of eastern Europe. The South Slavs were the ancestors of the modern Serbs, Croats, and Bosnians, while the Poles, Czechs, and Slovaks are descended from the West Slavs. The East Slavs, who settled the plains of northern Ukraine, Belarus, and the Moscow region in about A.D. 300, spread eastward and southward over the following centuries. In the ninth and tenth centuries, the Slavic peoples converted to Christianity.

Two brothers, Saint Cyril and Saint Methodius, translated the Bible into a Slavic language today known as Old Church Slavonic.

Kievan Rus'

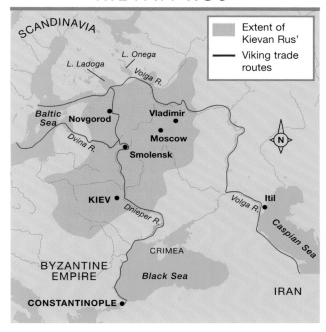

KIEVAN RUS'

Extent of Kievan Rus'
Viking trade routes

In the ninth and tenth centuries, the Slavs began to form principalities—territories ruled by powerful princes. The most powerful of these was a confederation of principalities known as Kievan Rus'. Although the ordinary people of Rus' were East Slavs, its leaders were Vikings from Scandinavia—known as Varangians.

By the ninth century, the territory occupied by the East Slavs straddled important trade routes between the Baltic and Black seas. Vikings sailed their ships up the Dvina and down the Dnieper and Volga rivers, trading furs, amber, and slaves. The Vikings also raided the wealthy empires of Byzantium and Iran that lay to the south. They made themselves masters of Slavic settlements such as Novgorod and Kiev.

One of the Viking adventurers, Rurik of Jutland (died about 879 A.D.), became prince of Novgorod in 862. His successor, Oleg, became ruler of Kiev in 882 and extended his power over a large area, known as Kievan Rus'. Rus', which was perhaps the name of Rurik's clan, gave its name to Russia, and Rurik's descendants—known as the Rurikid Dynasty—ruled Russia until 1598.

Under Vladimir I (956–1015), Kievan Rus' grew into one of the wealthiest territories in Europe. In 988, Vladimir persuaded the leader of the Greek Orthodox church in Constantinople—capital of the Byzantine

At its peak in the mid-11th century, Kievan Rus' extended from Lake Ladoga and Lake Onega in the north to the upper reaches of the Dnieper River.

The East Slavs who lived in the north came to be known as Russians, while those in the south were Ukrainians and Belorussians.

53

empire—to establish a cathedral in Kiev. This marked the foundation of the Russian Orthodox church. Vladimir also adopted other Byzantine ideas. He replaced the old clan structure of Russian society with a feudal one, controlled by an all-powerful ruler.

In the 11th century, rivalries between the various princes and shifting trade routes led to the breakup of Kievan Rus'. The most powerful principality was now Rostov-Suzdal, whose capital was Vladimir. One of the princes of Vladimir was Yuri Dolgoruky (1090–1157). Dolgoruky (Russian for "long arms") got his name owing to his habit of seizing the lands of neighboring princes. Yuri is also said to have been the founder of Moscow. In 1169, Yuri's son, Andrey Bogolyubov, sacked Kiev and moved the Russian court to Vladimir.

Alexander Nevsky

Alexander Nevsky (about 1220–1263) is one of Russia's greatest heroes. He was the son of a prince of Vladimir. In 1236, he was elected prince of Novgorod ("New Town"), which, despite its name, is Russia's oldest city. Under Nevsky, Novgorod reached the height of its power and prestige. In 1240, Prince Nevsky defeated the Swedes in a great battle on the Neva River, close to modern St. Petersburg, and earned his nickname "Nevsky." In 1246, he became grand duke of Kiev, and in 1252, the Mongol ruler Batu Khan made him Grand Prince of Vladimir. Nevsky's and his successors' diplomatic relations toward the Mongols helped Russia survive long years of foreign control.

The Golden Horde

In the 13th century, Russia was plundered by the Mongols—an army of Asiatic warriors led by the ruthless warlord, Genghis Khan (about 1162–1227). The Mongols, nomads who originally came from Mongolia in east Asia, were skilled horsemen and archers. After only a few decades, they established a vast empire that stretched almost the length and breadth of Asia. By the 1220s, Genghis's armies were pushing westward into Europe. The Slavs called the Mongolian invaders "Tatars."

In 1223, the Mongols won a victory over the Russian princes at the Battle of Kalka. In 1237, Batu Khan (died 1255), a grandson of Genghis, led a full-scale invasion of Russia. He sacked the towns of Moscow, Vladimir, Suzdal, and Kiev, and made their princes vassals of the Mongol empire. The Mongols did not occupy Rus'

THE GOLDEN HORDE

but demanded tribute, or taxes, and military service from the Russian princes and their subjects. Novgorod was saved because of floods, which prevented the Mongol armies from crossing the marshes surrounding the city.

Batu ruled a Mongol domain, or khanate, known as the Golden Horde. This extended from the Black and Caspian seas to the plains of western Siberia.

THE RISE OF MOSCOVY

In the shadow of the Mongols, Moscow and its surrounding territory—Moscovy—grew to be the most important of the Russian principalities. In 1380, Prince Dmitry of Moscow (1350–1389) led an alliance of Russian princes to victory against the Mongols at the Battle of Kulikovo on the Don River. Because of his triumph, Dmitry was honored with the surname Donskoy ("of the Don") and was made a saint of the Russian Orthodox church after his death.

The Mongols, however, fought back, and the Russian princes remained their vassals until 1480. Prince Ivan III, known as Ivan the Great (1440–1505), finally united almost all of the Russian principalities under his own rule. He tore up Moscow's treaty with the Mongols, whose empire was collapsing in any case, and stopped paying tribute.

The Mongol empire, ruled from its capital Karakorum, was divided into smaller areas called khanates. The Golden Horde was the most westerly and was ruled from the city of Sarai.

55

Ivan IV ruled Russia from 1547 to 1583. He is known as "the Terrible" because of the cruelty and ruthlessness that characterized his rule.

During the reigns of Ivan the Terrible, Peter the Great, and Catherine the Great, the Russian empire grew rapidly, swallowing up the homelands of many Asian peoples. By the mid-17th century, there were Russian cities on the shores of the Pacific.

Moscow's importance increased even more after the Muslim Turks sacked the Byzantine capital, Constantinople, in 1453. Moscow became the center of Orthodox Christianity. Ivan also married Sofia Palaeologus, a niece of the last Byzantine emperor.

Ivan the Terrible

Ivan the Great's grandson, Ivan IV (1530–1584), came to the throne when he was only three years old. His mother acted as regent, or temporary ruler, until he reached the age of 17, when he had himself crowned "Czar of All the Russias." Ivan IV was the first Russian ruler to claim this title.

Ivan was a brilliant soldier. He defeated the Mongol khanates of Kazan' and Astrakhan and expanded his empire south to the Caspian Sea and the Caucasus and east to the Yenisey River. To give thanks for these achievements, he built St. Basil's Cathedral in Moscow.

After the death of his beloved wife, however, Ivan IV became a bloodthirsty tyrant. He tortured and murdered

THE RUSSIAN EMPIRE

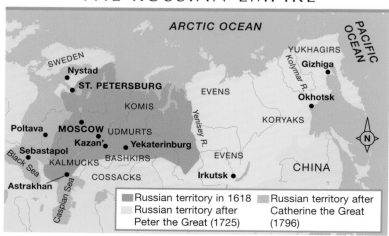

ARCTIC OCEAN

PACIFIC OCEAN

YUKHAGIRS

SWEDEN
Nystad
ST. PETERSBURG
Gizhiga
Kolyma R.
EVENS
Okhotsk
KOMIS
KORYAKS
Poltava
MOSCOW UDMURTS
Kazan'
Yekaterinburg
Yenisey R.
Sebastopol
EVENS
Black Sea
BASHKIRS
KALMUCKS
CHINA
Astrakhan
COSSACKS
Irkutsk
Caspian Sea
N

Russian territory in 1618
Russian territory after Peter the Great (1725)
Russian territory after Catherine the Great (1796)

Serfs and Cossacks

In medieval Europe, serfs were peasant farmers who were considered part of the land owned by the local lord. They were not much better than slaves. The very word *serf* comes from the Latin for "slave"—*servus.*

Serfs were forced to work their landlord's fields and, without his permission, could not travel or even marry. Russian serfs lived in dwellings called *izba*s, with log walls, thatched roofs, and a single room heated by a large, metal stove.

The situation of the serfs grew worse during the reign of Ivan the Terrible. Thousands of them escaped to the steppes to the south. There they formed self-governing communities and came to be known as Cossacks. The word *cossack* comes from a Turkic word, *kazak,* meaning "freeman" or "horseman."

The Cossacks were famous as courageous soldiers and fine horsemen. They wore distinctive uniforms with tall fur hats, sheepskin cloaks, baggy trousers, and knee boots.

The Russian czars treated the Cossacks very carefully, giving them their independence in return for occasional military service. The fierce-looking horseman shown here was one of many Cossacks who harried the troops of the French emperor Napoleon in 1812.

The Cossacks were always ready to show their proud, independent spirit and saw themselves as the protectors of the serfs. Stenka Razin (died 1671), a Cossack from the Don region, led a famous serf revolt against the Russian landowners in 1670. The largest Cossack uprising came in 1773, when the Cossack Yemelyan Pugachov (1726–1755) led thousands of serfs against the government. Pugachov captured the city of Kazan' and even

threatened Moscow before he was captured and executed. The serfs were finally freed by the Edict of Emancipation in 1861. The Cossacks gradually lost their independence and, by the late 19th century, were loyal to the czar.

Russian Dates

Our familiar system of measuring time is called the Gregorian calendar. It was named for Pope Gregory XIII, who devised it in the 16th century to correct inaccuracies in the older Julian calendar.

Gregory's reforms were taken up by most European countries and their colonies by the end of the 18th century. Russia had only started to use the Julian system in 1700 and did not change to the Gregorian calendar until 1918. By then, it was 14 days behind the rest of Europe. When the changeover was made, January 31, 1918, was followed the next day by February 14. This means that the anniversary of the October Revolution, which took place on October 25, 1917, is now commemorated on November 7.

To confuse things further, the Russian Orthodox church refuses to use the Gregorian system because it was devised by a Roman Catholic pope. Christmas Day in Russia is celebrated on January 7!

his opponents, formed Russia's first secret police, and even killed his own son and heir in a fit of rage. For these reasons, he became known as Ivan the Terrible.

The End of the Rurikid Dynasty

Ivan the Terrible died by poisoning in 1584 and was succeeded on the throne by his feeble second son, Fyodor. The latter was a poor ruler, and real power lay in the hands of his brother-in-law, Boris Godunov (about 1551–1605), an intelligent man who ruled wisely. During this period, Cossacks and fur traders led by the famous Stroganov family began to explore and settle Siberia.

When Fyodor died in 1598, he left no heir. Godunov took the throne, but his rule was plagued by a discontented nobility, known as the *boyars*. The *boyars* supported the cause of a Catholic impostor who claimed to be another son of Ivan the Terrible named Dmitry and the rightful heir to the throne. When Godunov died, the *boyars* murdered his son and installed the "False Dmitry" on the throne. The Rurikid dynasty was at an end, and Russia was plunged into the Time of Troubles—a period of chaos, violence, and foreign invasion.

Altogether, there were three "False Dmitrys," all of whom claimed to be Dmitry, the son of Ivan the Terrible.

THE ROMANOV DYNASTY

In 1613, a national congress elected Michael Romanov (1596–1645), a 16-year-old grandnephew of Ivan the Terrible, as the new czar of Russia. His descendants—the Romanovs—ruled Russia for the next three centuries. The first great czar of the Romanov dynasty was Michael's great-grandson, Peter I (1672–1725).

Peter the Great

Peter the Great, as he became known, was a huge man— 6 feet 7 inches (2.24 m) tall—with huge ambitions. Peter was the first Russian ruler to go outside Russia. He wanted to make Russia a great European nation like England, Spain, or France.

As a young man, Peter traveled through Germany, Holland, and England, studying the latest developments in industry, shipbuilding, and military technology. He is even said to have worked as a ship's carpenter in Amsterdam. On his return, he founded the Russian navy and forged a network of military alliances. His ambition was to expand Russian territory westward to the shores of the Baltic Sea. This would give Russia another valuable trading route. The other main route north through Arkhangel'sk was open only during the summer season when the Arctic Sea was briefly free of ice.

Russia's rival for possession of the Baltic territories was Sweden. In the Great Northern War, Russia allied itself with Poland and Denmark against Sweden. Russia won a brilliant victory against the Swedes at the Battle of Poltava (1709) and won the respect of all of Europe. The war ended finally in 1721, with the Treaty of Nystad, which gave Russia the eastern shores of the Baltic Sea.

To finance his reforms and military campaigns, Peter the Great imposed new taxes on his people. One of the most unpopular was the beard tax, which was designed not only to raise money but to encourage Russians to go clean-shaven like the Europeans. In this cartoon, the czar in European clothes wields a pair of scissors against the beard of a Russian nobleman.

The Great Northern Expedition

By the end of the 17th century, the Russian empire reached as far as the Pacific Ocean. At that time, the waters between America and Asia had not been fully explored. No one was quite sure whether Asia was linked by land to America or whether the continents were separated by sea.

Czar Peter the Great decided to find out the answer. His motive was to expand the Russian empire still further eastward into North America. In 1725, he launched an expedition under the leadership of the Dane Vitus Jonassen Bering (1681–1741). With a hundred

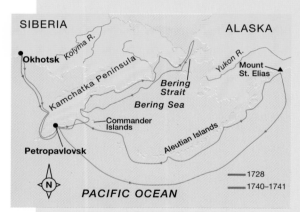

men, Bering made a six-month trek across Siberia to the Russian port of Okhotsk and onward by sea to Petropavlovsk, on Kamchatka.

In 1728, Bering set sail from Petropavlovsk in his ship, the *St. Gabriel*, and headed northeast. The czar's orders were that he should sail until either the

Siberian coast ran eastward—in which case Siberia was likely to be linked to America—or until he reached the mouth of the Kolyma River, in which case it was not. Bering reached as far north as the strait that today bears his name. The onset of winter, however, forced the *St. Gabriel* to turn back.

The czar was impressed enough to send Bering on another expedition to the east. This came to be known as the Great Northern Expedition, in which some 13,000 men took part. With such a large party, it took Bering eight years to reach the port of Okhotsk.

Finally, in June 1741, Bering set sail, this time heading east out to sea and landing in Alaska, close to Mount St. Elias. On the return voyage, storms forced Bering's ship, the *St. Peter*, to land on an island off Kamchatka. There Bering and 30 of his men died of scurvy and exposure. Survivors, however, brought back tales of the abundance of foxes, otters, and fur seals in Alaska.

In the following years, Russian fur traders set up settlements along the Alaskan coast. One settlement was called Novoarkhangel'sk, which later became Sitka, the Alaskan capital until 1900. A Russian outpost—Fort Russ (later Fort Ross)—was even set up in California in the early 19th century. The United States finally bought Alaska from Russia in 1867 for $7,200,000.

To mark his victory, Peter founded a new capital on the territory won from the Swedes and named it after his patron saint, Saint Peter—St. Petersburg. Not only was the new capital much closer to Europe than Moscow; it was built in a European style that recalled the great capitals of Western Europe, such as Venice, Amsterdam, and Paris.

Catherine the Great

By the end of his reign in 1725, Peter the Great had succeeded in his task of transforming Russia into a great European power. His work was continued by Catherine the Great (1729–1796).

Catherine was a German princess who came to Russia at age 16 to marry the heir to the throne—Peter, a relation of the Romanovs. She was ambitious and clever and embraced the ideas of the Enlightenment—an intellectual movement in Europe that believed people had the capacity to improve society through reason.

When her husband became czar as Peter III in 1762, Catherine and her supporters overthrew him. The new empress set about reforming the Russian state in the light of the new ideas from the West. She built new hospitals and schools, introduced a new legal code, and supported religious tolerance. Catherine did nothing, however, to improve the lot of the the vast majority of her people—the serfs. On the contrary, she crushed a huge serf rebellion led by the Cossack Yemelyan Pugachov.

Catherine also expanded the Russian empire, using a mixture of war and diplomacy. Present-day Belarus, eastern Poland, Lithuania, western Ukraine, and Crimea all came under Russian rule during this period.

Catherine the Great commissioned many artists to make portraits of her. The one above shows the empress as a great military leader, riding on horseback and with a sword in her hand.

The French Invasion of Russia

Catherine's favorite grandson took the throne as Alexander I (1777–1825) in 1801. His father, Paul I (1754–1801), had been murdered in a palace power struggle, and it was even rumored that Alexander was one of the plotters. Alexander I became famous as the czar who drove the French emperor Napoleon's army out of Russia.

By 1812, Napoleon had conquered much of western Europe, including Spain, Portugal, and northern Italy. In the summer of 1812, Napoleon led a huge army of 700,000 men eastward across the Russian plains. His goal was to capture Moscow. The Russians had only 350,000 soldiers with which to defend their country.

NAPOLEON'S INVASION

X Battle site

→ Advance of Napoleon's Grand Army

← Retreat of Napoleon's Grand Army

This map shows the advance and retreat of Napoleon's Grand Army during the 1812 invasion of Russia.

As the hopelessly outnumbered Russians retreated, they burned the crops in the fields. In September, they made a final stand at Borodino, 80 miles (130 km) west of Moscow. Thousands of soldiers from both armies died. The Russians retreated again, leaving Moscow undefended and allowing Napoleon to ride into the city unchallenged.

Waiting in Moscow for the czar to surrender, Napoleon ran out of time. Winter was approaching, there was not enough food, and his soldiers were 1,500 miles (2,400 km) from home. In October, Napoleon ordered a retreat. As the French made their long march back across the snow-covered plains, the Russians kept attacking them. Only one in twenty French soldiers survived.

Reform and Unrest

When Alexander I died in December 1825, a group of army officers held a rally in St. Petersburg. They were influenced by ideas from the rest of Europe and called for the abolition of serfdom and a more democratic form of government. The revolt was suppressed, and five of the so-called "Decembrists" were hanged for treason.

Under Alexander II (1818–1881; reigned 1855–1881), there were some attempts at reform. In 1861, the serfs were finally freed and given land of their own, although in return they had to make payments to their former landlords over 49 years. Very little was done to improve the life of the peasants. Many moved into the cities to find work in the new factories and on the railroads.

For many people, Alexander's reforms were not nearly enough. Some wanted Russia to develop peacefully into a democracy along the lines of the United States. A few favored more radical action. Students from the cities went into the countryside to rouse the peasants against their rulers. Others tried to encourage revolution among factory workers. Still others resorted to terrorism. In 1881, members of a secret society called the People's Will assassinated the czar, Alexander II.

A Bolshevik (Communist Party) poster shows the party leader, Vladimir Lenin, sweeping the emperors, priests, and capitalists off the face of the Earth.

Marxism

Many people who wanted change in Russia followed the political theories of the German Karl Marx (1818–1883). Marx's ideas, called Marxism, appeared in two very influential books: *The Communist Manifesto* (1848), written with Friedrich Engels, and *Capital* (1867).

Marx wrote that capitalism, the economic system based on private ownership and market forces, was unfair. It took wealth away from the working class—the people who created wealth through their labor—and concentrated it in the hands of a minority—the owners of businesses or factories.

According to Marxist teaching, capitalism was a necessary stage in the development of society, but it would later inevitably be replaced by communism. Under communism, all the wealth and resources of society would be jointly owned and shared by all the people.

REVOLUTION AND CIVIL WAR

Nicholas II (1868–1918)—the last of the Romanovs—came to the throne in 1894. Like his father, he resisted reform and refused to share his power with an elected assembly. He was also a poor diplomat. In 1904, he got Russia involved in a disastrous war with Japan. In 1905, the Japanese sank the whole of Russia's Baltic Fleet in the Tsushima Straits.

The 1905 Revolution

Meanwhile, the vast majority of the Russian people continued to live in deep poverty. In 1905, a priest named Georgy Gapon led a crowd of 200,000 striking workers and their families to the Winter Palace in St. Petersburg. They wanted to deliver a petition to Nicholas, whom they believed was kept in ignorance of the true condition of his country and people.

The czar's troops opened fire on the peaceful demonstrators and killed or injured hundreds of men, women, and children. The Bloody Sunday massacre shook the nation's faith in the czar and provoked a

The czar's Cossack troops charge against a crowd of demonstrating workers at the Winter Palace in St. Petersburg in 1905. The event—known as Bloody Sunday—sparked a nationwide wave of strikes, riots, and terrorist acts.

wave of riots, strikes, and peasant revolts throughout the country. In St. Petersburg harbor, there was a celebrated mutiny aboard the battleship *Potemkin*.

In the fall of 1905, the czar was finally forced to make some reforms. In his October Manifesto, he set up a limited elected assembly, called the Duma, and abolished the hated land payments. For the first time, peasants were able to buy up larger areas of land. This led to the emergence of a class of rich peasants called the *kulaks*.

Russia at War

For a time, it seemed that full-scale revolution had been avoided. Czar Nicholas II, however, became increasingly out of touch with his people, and he and his wife fell under the influence of a mysterious and fanatical "monk" named Grigory Rasputin (1872–1916; *see* box).

As an ally of France and Britain, Russia entered World War I in 1914 to fight against Austria and Germany. At first, the Russian army won victories against its enemies. Weak leadership, food shortages, and huge casualties, however, caused disillusionment and despair among the Russian people.

Another wave of riots and a revolt among army units stationed at Petrograd in 1917 finally persuaded the czar to abdicate (give up the throne). A provisional government under Prince Lvov took charge of the country.

Rasputin

In the early 1900s, a mysterious man appeared in St. Petersburg—Grigory Rasputin. Rasputin, a peasant from west Siberia, claimed to have had a vision of the Virgin Mary while working in the fields of the Russian countryside.

Rasputin's charisma and striking looks made him popular among the aristocratic women of St. Petersburg. Eventually, the czarina Alexandra summoned him to court. She believed that he was able to cure her son, Alexis, of an inherited blood condition called hemophilia. Apparently successful, Rasputin gained influence over the whole royal family, including the czar. He became very unpopular when people blamed him for the disasters of World War I.

Eventually, a group of Russian aristocrats decided to rid Russia of Rasputin. They invited him to dinner and poisoned his food and wine. Rasputin ate and drank greedily but seemed immune to the poison. The plotters had to beat and shoot him before he was thrown into the freezing Neva River.

In 1914, the Russian capital, St. Petersburg, was renamed Petrograd because St. Petersburg was considered a German name.

Lenin

Vladimir Ilyich Lenin (1870–1924) was one of the most important political figures of the 20th century. He was the founder of the Russian Communist Party, the leader of the Russian Revolution, and the founder and first head of the USSR—the world's largest country.

Lenin was born in Simbirsk, 400 miles east of Moscow. His real name was Vladimir Ilyich Ulyanov. After his elder brother, Alexander, was hanged for plotting to assassinate the czar, Lenin became a Marxist revolutionary. In 1895, he was jailed for his activities and, in 1897, was exiled to Siberia. In 1900, he began to call himself "Lenin," after the Lena River in eastern Siberia. In 1905, he left Russia to join other revolutionaries in western Europe.

From outside Russia, Lenin directed the activities of the Bolsheviks. In 1917, he returned secretly to Petrograd to lead the October Revolution. "History will not forgive us," he told his fellow party members, "if we do not assume power now."

Lenin did not remain long in power. His health was shattered by the revolution and war. In 1924, he died and his body was placed in a tomb in Red Square. Many Russians still revere the memory of Lenin. This portrait (below) was made in 1990 to celebrate Lenin Victory Day. After the fall of the Soviet Union in 1991, there were calls to remove Lenin's body from his tomb and to bury him close to his mother in Simbirsk.

The October Revolution

In 1898, Russian revolutionary Marxists formed the Russian Social Democratic Party. The party's objective was to overthrow the czar, but it was quickly split by a disagreement over how this aim should be achieved.

The majority of party members called for an immediate revolution led by the party elite. They were known as the *Bolsheviks* (meaning "majority"). The leader of this hardline faction was Vladimir Ilyich Lenin *(see* box). His less radical opponents—the *Mensheviks* ("minority")— wanted to build up a mass party, which would come to power by force of numbers. After the failed 1905 Revolution, Lenin and other revolutionaries fled abroad.

Although Nicholas II abdicated on March 1, 1917, the provisional government refused to take Russia out of the war. In April, Lenin and other exiled Bolsheviks secretly returned to Russia to start unrest in the workers' councils—known in Russian as "soviets." There were a few demonstrations, but they were crushed, and Lenin escaped back to Finland.

In September, the Russian army sent soldiers to crush the soviet in Petrograd. This brutal act turned public opinion in favor of the Bolsheviks. Lenin saw his chance to seize power and returned to Petrograd to organize the revolution. On the night of October 24–25, 1917, a blank shell fired from the battleship *Aurora*, moored in the Neva River, gave the signal to begin the storming of the Winter Palace—the seat of the provisional government. Bolshevik workers and soldiers from the Petrograd Soviet occupied the city's public buildings, arrested the government, and took power in an almost bloodless coup.

Soon, Soviets took control in industrial towns and cities across the country. In Moscow, however, there were ten days of street fighting before the revolutionaries gained the upper hand.

"All power to the Soviets."
—Bolshevik slogan just before the revolution.

Under the communists, the battleship Aurora *became a powerful symbol of the revolution. During World War II, the Russians sank the ship in order to protect it from German bombs. Today, the* Aurora *is a museum.*

The Fate of the Romanovs

After the October Revolution, the Bolsheviks held the former czar Nicholas II, his wife, Alexandra, and their five children under house arrest in the city of Yekaterinburg, just east of the Urals.

At first, the communist government planned to put Nicholas on trial for crimes against the people. However, in July 1918, as the White Army threatened to capture the city, Lenin ordered the royal family to be executed.

The Romanovs, their doctor, and three servants were shot, and their bodies were burned and thrown into a pit. Their remains were discovered in 1991. Scientists used DNA tests to prove that the bones truly belonged to the czar and his family.

There had been rumors that Anastasia, the czar's youngest daughter, had survived. A woman named Anna Anderson, who appeared in Berlin in 1920, convinced many people that she was Anastasia. Anderson died in the United States in 1984, but DNA evidence proved she had been an imposter.

The remains of the family were finally laid to rest in the Peter and Paul Cathedral in St. Petersburg—the traditional burial place of the Romanov dynasty—in 1998 (below). The mourners held religious icons as well as portraits of the czar. Many Russians revere the memory of the last czar. Some even argue that the royal family should be restored to the throne.

Civil War

The Bolsheviks promptly made peace with Germany by signing the Treaty of Brest-Litovsk in March 1918. Under the treaty, Russia gave up territory in Ukraine, Poland, the Baltic, and Finland. The government also abolished the private ownership of land. Within six months, the Bolsheviks had renamed themselves the Communist Party, moved the Russian capital back to Moscow, and set up the Cheka (secret police), a forerunner of the notorious national security force, the KGB.

CIVIL WAR

Area controlled by Bolsheviks October 1919
- - - Boundary of Russian empire 1914
→ Attacks by Western powers
→ Attacks by White Russians
→ Attacks by other nationalities

Not everyone in Russia supported the revolution. Supporters of the czar joined other opponents of the Bolsheviks to form what was called the White Army. Leon Trotsky (1879–1940), one of Lenin's comrades, took command of the Red Guards, who had helped the Bolsheviks take power, and transformed them into the disciplined and effective Red Army. Three years of bloody civil war followed. The Cheka also ruthlessly suppressed dissent and terrorized enemies of the revolution. It imprisoned or executed anyone suspected of counterrevolutionary activities.

White resistance was eventually crushed. About 1.5 million White Russians—mostly educated, upper and middle-class people—escaped from the country. Many went to France; some settled in the United States. By 1921, the communists had firmly established a one-party, or totalitarian, state. Lenin also announced a New Economic Policy (NEP), which allowed some private enterprise, to rebuild the shattered country. As the economy began to recover, Soviet politics took on a new and sinister direction.

After the revolution, the survival of the new communist country was threatened by both civil war and invasion. While White Russians attempted to seize back territory from the Bolsheviks, Britain, France, United States, and some neighboring countries launched invasions from all sides.

"Peace, land, and bread."
—Bolshevik slogan

THE RULE OF STALIN

In 1922, Lenin suffered a stroke, and he was effectively removed from power. He died two years later and was followed as leader by Joseph Stalin, the general secretary of the Communist Party. Lenin's favored successor was Trotsky. Stalin got the better of Trotsky, however, and expelled him from the party in 1927. Trotsky escaped abroad in 1929, but one of Stalin's agents tracked him down in Mexico in 1940 and murdered him with an ice pick.

Joseph Stalin

Russia's most feared leader, Joseph Stalin (1879–1953), was born Iosef Vissarionovich Dzugashvili in Gori, Georgia. The son of a poor shoemaker and a laundress, he joined the Bolsheviks in 1903 and became an enthusiastic follower of Lenin. Like his hero, he changed his name, choosing Stalin, from the Russian word *stal*, meaning "steel."

In 1912, Stalin became the first editor of the Bolshevik party newspaper, *Pravda* ("Truth"). Although lacking in charisma, he was a hard worker and expert organizer. After the revolution, he served in a number of minor government posts. Appointed the party's general secretary in 1922, he quickly began to build himself a power base.

The Soviet Union

During the civil war, the Red Army had occupied much of the territory lost under the terms of the Treaty of Brest-Litovsk. Stalin forced the new Soviet republics on the fringes of Russia—Belarus, Ukraine, and Transcaucasia—into federation with the Russian Republic to form the Union of Soviet Socialist Republics (USSR) in December 1922. By 1940, the USSR also included the Central Asian republics of Kazakhstan, Turkmenistan, Kirghizstan, Uzbekistan, and Tajikistan, and the Baltic states of Estonia, Latvia, and Lithuania.

The Five-Year Plans

War and revolution had left Russia economically devastated. The country's wealth was still rooted in its agriculture—some 80 percent of the population were peasants. Stalin, however, wanted to transform the country into a mighty industrial power that would be able to compete with the capitalist economies of coun-

Between 1928 and 1940, Russia's steel production increased four-fold; and it produced 30 times more tractors.

tries such as the United States, Britain, and France. To do so, he carried out a series of economic plans, each of which lasted five years.

The first Five-year Plan, launched in 1929, aimed to double Russia's industrial output. Numerous new mines, giant steelworks, and factories were built, particularly in Siberia, and strict production quotas were set. A hard-working miner named Aleksey Stakhanov (1905–1977) was promoted as a Soviet hero in an attempt to encourage efficiency.

Stalin also needed more food in order to feed the growing urban workforce. He forced the peasants to pool their land into collective farms, or *kolkhozy*, and aimed to increase agricultural produce by half.

Many peasants resisted the changes, especially in the good agricultural land of Ukraine and the Volga–Don region. Thousands of those who resisted were shot or sent to labor camps. In 1932, a terrible drought developed. Instead of sending aid to the areas affected by drought, Stalin demanded that they continue to send their grain quotas to the government. One of the worst famines in living memory was the result. Some six million people starved to death.

Both industry and agriculture failed to meet Stalin's ambitious targets. Nevertheless, by 1938 the Soviet Union was one of the biggest industrial nations in the world, second only to the United States.

The Great Terror

Faced with growing unrest both among the people and party members, Stalin began to purge, or remove, everyone in a

During the Soviet Union, workers were heroes. A statue of an Industrial Laborer and a Collective Farm Girl (below) stood on top of the Soviet Pavilion at the International Exhibition held in Paris in 1937. The tools held by the two figures together make up the Soviet symbol— the hammer and sickle (left).

position of power or responsibility who dared to show the slightest opposition to his policies. Calling them "enemies of the people," Stalin used them as scapegoats for everything that was wrong with the Soviet economy and society. In a series of purges, the "enemies of the people" were arrested and shipped off to the Gulag (see box).

At the height of the purges in 1936, Stalin's former Bolshevik comrades, Lev Kamenev and Grigory Zinoviev, the Red Army chief of staff, Marshal Mikhail Tukhachevsky, and other important people were forced to appear at show trials. Here they were force to confess publicly to their "crimes" and were taken away and shot. Altogether some 8.5 million Soviet officials and ordinary citizens were jailed, exiled, or executed during the Terror.

The Gulag

The Gulag was a network of labor camps set up in 1930 by the Russian secret police. The word is short for *Glavnoe Upravlenie Isparvitelno-Trudovykh Lagerey*, meaning "Chief Administration of Corrective Labor Camps." The Gulag camps were scattered through the remote regions of northern Russia, Siberia, and the Russian Far East. They were so far from settled areas that escape was almost impossible. People who did escape perished in the severe cold or starved to death in the wilderness.

People imprisoned in the Gulag included peasants and farmers who resisted collectivization; writers and artists who criticized the Communist Party; party members who fell out of favor with Stalin; and anyone who was suspected of being disloyal to the Soviet state.

The inmates endured cold, hunger, and hardship and were forced to do heavy labor in terrible conditions. As many as 15 million people served long sentences in the Gulag, and most of them died there. In 1991, after the fall of the Soviet Union, the new president, Boris Yeltsin, released the last ten Gulag prisoners.

The Great Patriotic War

For Russians, World War II is referred to as the Great Patriotic War. In 1939, Britain and France tried to persuade Stalin to ally with them against Nazi Germany. Stalin refused and instead signed a pact with the German leader, Adolf Hitler. Under the pact, Russia and Germany agreed not to go to war with each other and to divide Poland between them. Communists throughout the world were shocked by the pact between Soviet Russia and Nazi Germany. Stalin, they felt, had betrayed the cause of communism. In reality, Stalin wanted time to build up his army in preparation for war.

Hitler, too, had no intention of keeping the pact with Stalin. On June 22, 1941, in Operation Barbarossa, Germany invaded Russia. The Red Army was still ill-prepared for the German attack. By the fall, the Germans had reached Moscow and were laying siege to Leningrad, as Petrograd was now called in honor of Lenin.

The harsh Russian winter gave the Red Army time to regroup. In a wave of patriotic feeling, the entire Soviet Union swung behind the war effort. Tractor factories started manufacturing tanks. Women labored in munitions plants, worked as nurses and radio operators, or even fought as soldiers. Every fit man was sent to the front.

Deportation

During the 1920s, the Soviet regime began to forcibly move (deport) non-Russian minorities living on its frontiers to Siberia and Central Asia. During the war, suspicion of these peoples became rife, and Stalin ordered mass deportations of entire races. In total, some 3.5 million people made up of 50 nationalities were deported during the war. In the 1990s, President Boris Yeltsin apologized for the deportations, blaming them for the interethnic conflict that blighted the new Russian Federation.

Victory!

The fighting was hard and bitter, with huge casualties on both sides. The turning point came on February 2, 1943, with the Battle of Stalingrad, when what was left of Hitler's Sixth Army surrendered. The Germans were driven out of Russia, and the victorious Red Army entered Berlin, the German capital, in April 1945.

The war took an enormous toll on the Soviet Union. Experts estimate that 26 million Soviet citizens were killed, and millions more were maimed and injured. The western

This Russian poster was published in 1942 to promote the wartime alliance between the Soviet Union, the United States, and Britain. A Red Army soldier leads his U.S. and British comrades across the body of the German leader, Adolf Hitler.

parts of the Soviet Union were devastated; 1,700 towns and cities and 70,000 villages had been destroyed, farms lay in ruins, and hardly a factory was left standing.

In an agreement reached at Yalta in February 1945 by Stalin, British Prime Minister Winston Churchill, and U.S. President Franklin D. Roosevelt, the three countries agreed to govern those regions they occupied at the end of the war until free elections could be held. By the spring of 1945, the Red Army occupied eastern Germany, Poland, Czechoslovakia, Romania, Bulgaria, Albania, and Hungary. Instead of allowing free elections, however, the Soviet Union helped bring local communist parties to power.

During the Cold War, Europe was largely divided between the communist countries of the east, allied with the Soviet Union, and the capitalist countries of the west, allied with the United States. A few countries remained neutral.

THE COLD WAR PERIOD

After World War II, there was a long period of tension between the USSR and the West, in particular the United States. Each side mistrusted the other. The United States and its allies feared that communism would spread throughout the world; Russia believed that the West was plotting to overthrow the Soviet government. The rivalry and mistrust always threatened to break out as a direct military conflict. The Cold War intensified after the Soviets developed a nuclear bomb of their own in 1949. A dangerous and expensive arms race began between the two "superpowers," the United States and the Soviet Union, in which each side tried to develop more military power than the other.

A DIVIDED EUROPE

Soviet bloc
Western bloc
Neutral

ICELAND
FINLAND
NORWAY
SWEDEN
THE NETHERLANDS
IRELAND
DENMARK
MOSCOW •
UNITED KINGDOM
EAST GERMANY
SOVIET UNION
• BERLIN
WEST GERMANY
POLAND
BELGIUM LUXEMBOURG
CZECHOSLOVAKIA
AUSTRIA
HUNGARY
FRANCE
ROMANIA
SWITZERLAND
YUGOSLAVIA
PORTUGAL
ITALY
BULGARIA
SPAIN
ALBANIA
TURKEY
GREECE

The Space Race

During the Cold War, the United States and the USSR competed to be the first to develop space technology. Both countries spent millions of dollars as scientists raced to put the first artificial satellite into orbit around the Earth.

The Russians beat the Americans by almost four months, launching *Sputnik 1* on October 4, 1957. The first American satellite, *Explorer 1*, was launched on January 31, 1958. Sputnik continued to orbit the Earth every 96 minutes until early 1958, when it burned up on re-entering the Earth's atmosphere. *Sputnik 2* was bigger than *Sputnik 1* and carried a dog named Laika into space.

The Russians also won the race to put the first human into space. The *Vostok 1* space capsule blasted off on April 12, 1961, carrying Yuri Gagarin (1934–1968) into orbit less than a month before Alan Shepard became the first American in space. Gagarin returned to a hero's welcome. He was killed a few years later when his jet aircraft crashed during a training flight. The first woman in space was also Russian—Valentina Tereshkova orbited the Earth in *Vostok 6* in 1963.

Soviet successes in space spurred the United States to speed up its own program. The rivalry with the Soviets was called the Space Race. There were even different words for people in space. The American equivalent of a Russian *cosmonaut* was an astronaut.

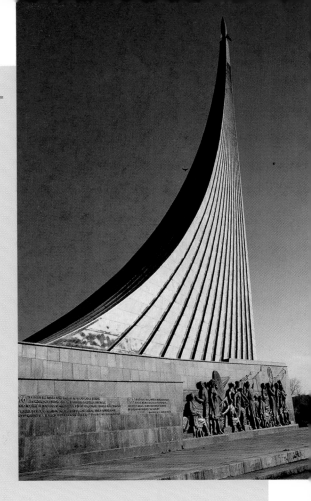

In 1961, President John F. Kennedy committed the United States "before the decade is out, to land a man on the moon and return him safely to earth." The United States won the race to the Moon in 1969, and, in fact, the Russians have never landed on Earth's satellite.

The soaring obelisk shown above is the monument to Soviet space exploration in Moscow. It is 328 feet (100 m) high and is made out of titanium—a very strong but light element that is often used in building spacecraft. Beneath the obelisk is the Museum of Cosmonautics (space travel).

The KGB

The Russian secret police, the KGB, was founded in 1954 and developed out of earlier agencies such as the Cheka and the MGB ("Ministry for State Security"). The KGB's initials stood for *Komitet Gosudarstvennoy Bezopasnosti*, Russian for the "Committee for State Security." Under Stalin, the MGB had become one of the USSR's most feared and hated organizations. It was responsible for the arrest, imprisonment, and execution of thousands of Soviet citizens suspected of holding anticommunist views.

The formation of the KGB was an attempt to change the image of the secret police. Like its predecessors, however, the ruling administration used the KGB to keep control of the country. Some 300,000 KGB troops were responsible for keeping watch over the USSR's borders, and preventing citizens from leaving or intruders from entering its territory. Another important role of the KGB was the gathering of international intelligence and, as such, it was an important weapon in the Cold War. The KGB was disbanded in 1991.

After Stalin

When Stalin died in 1953, Nikita Sergeyevich Khrushchev (1894–1971) took over. During his term as leader up to 1964, there was hope that things would improve both at home and abroad. New mining projects and oil drilling rigs began to exploit the untapped natural resources of Siberia, and new cities, roads, and railroads were built. Great Soviet technological achievements of this time included the *Sputnik* satellite launch and Yuri Gagarin's space flight (*see* p. 75). Khrushchev also permitted greater cultural freedom. In 1962, the administration allowed the writer Alexander Solzhenitsyn to publish his powerful story about the brutality of Stalin's labor camps, *A Day in the Life of Ivan Denisovich*.

It was Khrushchev, however, who was responsible for the most dangerous moment of the Cold War. In 1962, he stationed nuclear missiles in Cuba, within striking range of American cities. For a while, the U.S. president at the time, John F. Kennedy, considered launching an air attack on the Cuban missile sites. The world was on the brink of nuclear war when the White House received news from Moscow that Khrushchev had agreed to withdraw the missiles.

Leonid Brezhnev (1906–1982) replaced Khrushchev as leader in 1964. Under his rule, Russia entered a period of stability and prosperity. People received a good education and were reasonably sure of keeping their jobs. Nevertheless, the government kept tight control of society. There was no freedom of expression, and organizations such as unions were forbidden. Very few people were free to travel outside the Soviet Union.

Many Russians were unhappy with the situation in their country, but only a few dared to speak out. The most famous dissident, as these brave people were known, was the physicist and human-rights campaigner Andrey Sakharov, who was exiled to Gorky (now Nizhniy Novgorod) in 1980. Other dissidents suffered harsher treatment and were sent to labor camps.

Although conditions within the Soviet Union were terrible, relations with the West improved. In 1972, U.S. president Richard Nixon met with Brezhnev in Moscow and signed the Strategic Arms Limitation Treaty (SALT), which slowed the nuclear arms race.

Andrey Sakharov (1928–1989) helped build the Soviet Union's first hydrogen bomb. He later founded the Committee for Human Rights and, in 1975, was awarded the Nobel Peace Prize.

Glasnost' and the End of the Cold War

When a new president, Mikhail Gorbachev (born 1931), came to power in 1985, he cleared the government of older communists with fixed, old ideas and replaced them with younger men like himself. He introduced new policies of *glasnost'*, or "openness," and of *perestroika*, or "restructuring," in an attempt to revitalize the Soviet economy and society, and encourage free enterprise.

THE END OF THE SOVIET UNION

In 1991, the non-Russian republics of the former Soviet Union declared their independence. The Russian Republic later became the Russian Federation. Most of the former Soviet republics subsequently joined the Commonwealth of Independent States (CIS).

Boris Yeltsin waves the white, blue, and red Russian flag— banned under the Soviet regime—during the attempted communist coup of 1991. Yeltsin used the flag as a way of appealing to the rising tide of national pride (nationalism) among the Russian people.

Gorbachev also traveled abroad, trying to convince the West that Russia was no longer a threat. He agreed on major cuts in nuclear weapons with the U.S. president Ronald Reagan. He released thousands of political prisoners and, in 1989, held the first free national election in Russia since 1917.

As repression eased and the Communist Party's grip on power became less strong, the Soviet satellite states in Eastern Europe demanded independence. One by one, the communist regimes in Poland, Hungary, East Germany, Czechoslovakia, Bulgaria, and Romania were overthrown. The reunification of Germany on October 3, 1990, marked the end of the Cold War.

Many old-style communists were unhappy with the turn of events. In August 1991, a number of them attempted to overthrow Gorbachev. Boris Yeltsin (*see* box opposite), a popular politician who had recently been elected president of the Russian Republic, rallied opposition to the coup at Moscow's White House, the seat of the Russian parliament. In one of the more famous scenes in recent Russian history, Yeltsin climbed on top of a tank to deliver a speech declaring the coup illegal. Huge crowds filled the streets in Moscow and Leningrad to support Yeltsin, and the coup collapsed.

In the months following the August coup, demands for independence from the Soviet republics within the USSR marked the end of the Soviet Union. On December 25, 1991, Gorbachev resigned, and the white, blue, and red flag of Russia replaced the red Soviet flag above the dome of the Kremlin's Senate House.

A NEW COUNTRY

In December 1991, the Soviet Union was dissolved and was replaced by a group of independent republics—Russia, Ukraine, Belarus, Moldova, Estonia, Latvia, Lithuania, Georgia, Armenia, Azerbaijan, Kazakhstan, Turkmenistan, Uzbekistan, Kyrgyzstan, and Tajikistan. All of these except the Baltic countries of Estonia, Latvia, and Lithuania joined the newly formed Commonwealth of Independent States (CIS), a loose alliance of former Soviet republics.

Yeltsin Becomes President

Boris Yeltsin became president of the newly independent Russian Republic in 1991. He set about enacting a series of radical reforms to convert Russia from its state-owned, planned economy to a free-market, capitalist system.

At first, the Russian people welcomed the reforms. The new freedoms, however, were accompanied by increased crime and falling living standards. In 1993, communists belonging to the National Salvation Front occupied the White House and attempted a revolt. Yeltsin ordered soldiers to fire on the building, and almost 150 people were killed.

Yeltsin also faced opposition from the non-Russian regions of the republic, who began to demand more independence. Fearing that the republic, like the Soviet Union before it, was going to disintegrate, parliament approved a new constitution in 1993. This gave the regions more independence and reshaped the Russian republic as the Russian Federation.

Boris Yeltsin

The dominant figure in Russia during the 1990s was Boris Yeltsin. As president for most of the decade, Yeltsin oversaw a turbulent period in Russian history, as the country attempted to throw off the shackles of communism.

Yeltsin was born in 1931 and joined the Communist Party in 1961. During the 1980s, he became increasingly dissatisfied with the slowness of Mikhail Gorbachev's economic reforms, and he resigned from the party in 1990. Despite deteriorating physical and mental health, Yeltsin held on to power until December 31, 1999, when he gave Russians new cause for optimism by announcing his resignation. He was replaced by Vladimir Putin.

"Freedom is... like air. When you have it, you don't notice it."
—Boris Yeltsin

RUSSIA'S ADMINISTRATION

Like the United States, the Russian Federation is a democratic federal republic. The parliament is called the Federal Assembly and has two chambers—the Council of the Federation and the State Duma. The Council of the Federation, or upper house, has 178 deputies. Two deputies are appointed from each of the federation's 89 administrative sectors.

The State Duma, or lower house, has 450 deputies. Half of the Duma deputies are elected for a four-year term using a "first past the post" system in which the person with most votes wins. This means that losing candidates have no representation even if they have had nearly as many votes. The other half are chosen from party lists by proportional representation. The Duma sits in a former Soviet building near the Kremlin.

The head of state is the president, who is elected by the people for a four-year term and cannot preside for more than two terms together. His offices are in the Kremlin. The president is very powerful. He can issue

*The Russian
administration is still
evolving, and the new
constitution, which
came into force in
1993, is likely to
change over the
coming years.
At present, the
constitution
concentrates a great
deal of power in the
hands of the president.*

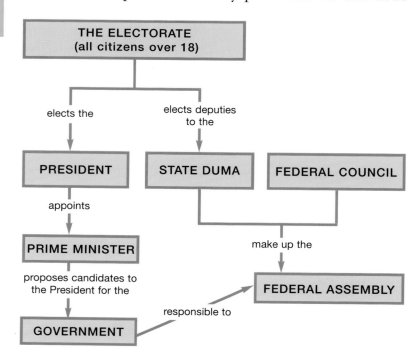

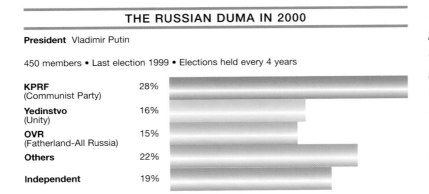

THE RUSSIAN DUMA IN 2000

President Vladimir Putin

450 members • Last election 1999 • Elections held every 4 years

KPRF (Communist Party)	28%
Yedinstvo (Unity)	16%
OVR (Fatherland-All Russia)	15%
Others	22%
Independent	19%

This chart shows the proportion of seats shared by the political parties in 2000, following the election in December 1999. In total, 26 parties took part in the election.

decrees—laws that do not have to be voted on in the Duma. He is also in charge of defense, security, and foreign policy. The head of government is the prime minister, who is appointed by the president. Some of the ministers who serve in the government report directly to the president rather than to the prime minister. These include the ministers for defense, foreign affairs, home affairs, and television and radio (the media).

The Political Parties

During the Soviet period, only one political party was allowed to exist in Russia—the Communist Party—which was always in charge of the government. This meant that the roles of the Communist Party and the government were not very distinct.

Today, there are dozens of political parties, and many of these are represented in the Duma. The Communist Party remains a very powerful political force in Russia. Other important parties are the moderate *Yedinstvo* ("Unity"), the nationalist Fatherland-All Russia bloc, the extreme nationalist Liberal Democratic Party, and *Yabloko*, which supports the market economy.

Russia's White House

Moscow's White House was built during the 1970s as the administrative headquarters of the Russian Republic—then part of the Soviet Union. In 1990, the building became the seat of the republic's first elected congress—headed by Boris Yeltsin—and the focus of the people's calls for reform. It was here that, in August 1991, Yeltsin went to rally opposition to an attempted hard-line communist coup. As soon as Yeltsin became president, however, the White House congress became a source of opposition to his rule. In 1993, the White House was occupied by communists. Yeltsin ordered troops to storm the parliament, killing some 150 people.

The Economy

"What is the essence of perestroika, I ask, and I get a sarcastic answer: They want to work in the new way provided everything remains just as it has always been."

Soviet commentator B. Mozhayev

Russia has an extraordinary abundance of energy and mineral resources. Throughout this vast country are rich reserves of coal, oil, gas, and iron ore. There are fast-running rivers to generate hydroelectricity, and the Ural Mountains are a treasure-house of metal ores, including gold, nickel, and copper. The country also possesses the largest area of forest in the world.

During the communist period, the government controlled almost every part of the economy. Private businesses were illegal, and all factories, farms, and shops were owned by the government. Using this system, Russia's leaders transformed the Soviet Union from a backward, agricultural nation into an industrial giant that was second only to the United States.

In the late 20th century, amid the chaos that followed the fall of Soviet communism, Russia's economic might went into rapid decline. By 1997, Russia's industrial output—the amount of manufactured goods it produced—was only the 13th largest in the world, behind that of many smaller countries, such as France, Spain, and South Korea.

The new Russian leaders have introduced a Western-style, free-market economy in the hope of reviving the country's fortunes. They are working to bring government-owned businesses into private ownership and have looked to countries such as the United States and Japan for help with Russia's industries.

Russian industry often has to contend with severe weather conditions, such as the long winter freeze. This ice-bound construction site is in Yakutsk, Siberia.

FACT FILE

- Russia is the third-largest producer of crude oil in the world. Most of its oilfields are located in western Siberia.

- Russia is among the world's top ten producers of gold, copper, nickel, and aluminum.

- After the United States, Russia is the world's largest producer of energy. However, it is also among the least efficient users of energy in the world. As a nation, its energy efficiency is about 4 percent of that of Switzerland, the most efficient.

- The Trans-Siberian Railroad is the longest railroad in the world. It stretches for 5,786 miles (9,311 km).

Russia's economy is dependent on industry and services. Since the fall of the Soviet Union, unemployment has been very high, running at some 11 percent in 1997.

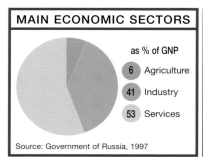

MAIN ECONOMIC SECTORS

as % of GNP

6	Agriculture
41	Industry
53	Services

Source: Government of Russia, 1997

THE WORKFORCE

% of workforce

13.3	Agriculture
41.3	Industry
45.4	Services

Source: Government of Russia, 1997

During the Soviet era, the government urged women to take jobs outside the home. This Soviet poster tells mothers about the state-run child care that allowed them to work in the new factories.

FROM COMMUNISM TO CAPITALISM

Russia's transformation from the communist dictatorship of the Soviet era to a modern, Western-style economy based on free competition between businesses has threatened to tear the country apart. Under the Soviet system, the economy was planned centrally—that is, it was the government, rather than businesspeople, who set production targets and decided on the most effective way to run the economy. There was very little private enterprise. The government owned all the land and heavy industry and ran large farms called collectives.

When the Soviet Union was dissolved in 1991, President Boris Yeltsin was determined that the new Russia would make a fast change to a free-market economy. However, the lack of investment, inefficient tax collection, and widespread crime and corruption that dogged the early years of the Russian Federation left the economy in chaos. The value of Russia's currency—the ruble—crashed from 50 rubles to the U.S. dollar in 1991 to 6,000 to the dollar by 1997. In 1998, a differently valued ruble was introduced, with new bills. In

Russians stand in line for food outside a shop in Moscow. Shortages of food, services, and manufactured goods are commonplace in Russian cities.

1997, Russia's gross national product per capita—the value of goods produced per head of population—was just $2,680 per person. The United States' was $29,080.

As a result of this economic collapse, the Russian people have had to put up with joblessness, food shortages, high prices, and financial hardship. Nevertheless, despite having to live with such economic uncertainties, most people still support the reforms.

Minerals and Energy

Russia's vast wealth of minerals includes deposits of iron ore, gold, copper, nickel, lead, zinc, and diamonds (*see* box). The majority of these deposits are located in Siberia. The remoteness, severe climate, and difficult terrain of this region make it difficult to exploit these resources.

After the United States, Russia is the world's biggest producer of energy. The country has abundant reserves of coal, oil, and gas. There are important coal fields in the Urals, in eastern Siberia, at Vorkuta in the

Distant Treasures

Russian geologists have calculated that the Ural Mountains contain more than 20,000 different minerals, including rich deposits of precious and semiprecious stones. The Hermitage Museum in St. Petersburg contains many beautiful objects made from semiprecious stones. These include the Malachite Hall, a room that is decorated from floor to ceiling with malachite—a bright-green copper ore.

Large diamond deposits were discovered in the Yakutia region of Siberia in the 1950s. A new city, Mirnyy, was built to house the mine workers. Mirnyy is very remote and can be reached only by airplane. Today, Russia produces a quarter of all the world's diamonds.

Pollution

One of the major problems that the Russian Federation has inherited from the Soviet Union is pollution. The development of heavy industry meant that by the 1970s, many areas of the country were severely affected by air and water pollution, deforestation, and soil erosion and contamination. The map below shows where the most serious environmental problems facing the Russian Federation are today.

Russia is currently losing some 370,000–445,000 acres (150,000 to 180,000 ha) of woodland each year, owing to the effects of acid rain, logging, and forest fires. Rivers and lakes have been so polluted and damaged by dam-building that many unique fish species are now extinct. The most serious areas of environmental damage are in the industrial zones of the Urals and European Russia. In many Russian cities, pollution is five times above internationally acceptable limits.

Most serious of all is the threat of radioactive pollution. The Soviet navy dumped some 17,000 contaminated containers into the Barents Sea. At the naval base of Polyarny, near Murmansk, old nuclear submarines lie rusting in their berths because there is not enough money to dispose of their nuclear reactors safely.

In fact, the major problem with many of Russia's environmental issues is money. The Russian government does not have the financial resources to pay to clean up the hazards.

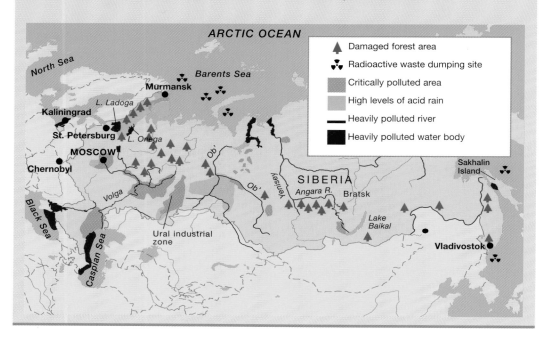

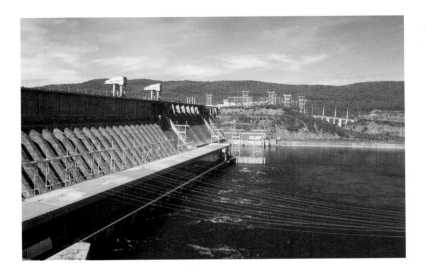

Siberia's wide-open spaces and large rivers have made it a suitable area for hydroelectric plants, such as this one on the Yenisey River in Siberia. Increasingly, however, people are unhappy with the environmental damage that such projects can cause.

Arctic, and in the Kuznetsk Basin. There are also huge oil deposits in western Siberia; Russia was one of the first countries in the world to develop an oil industry.

Russia is the world's number one producer of natural gas and has around 40 percent of the world's reserves. The main gas and oil fields are in the Volga–Urals region, the northern Caucasus, and western Siberia. A vast network of pipelines built in the 1970s and 1980s links these areas to European Russia.

Hydroelectric projects, which harness the power of rivers by storing water in artificially created reservoirs, generate almost 19 percent of Russia's energy output. Important hydroelectric plants can be found on the Volga, Ob', Yenisey, and Angara rivers. The Bratsk hydroelectric plant on Siberia's Angara River is one of the biggest in the world. Completed in 1964, the plant's dam holds back the world's second-largest artificial lake, which is more than 200 miles (320 km) long.

Russia is one of the world's largest producers of nuclear power. Many of the country's nuclear reactors are out of date, and some people consider them unsafe. In support of their argument is the fact that the world's worst nuclear disaster took place at Chernobyl in 1986, in Ukraine, which was then part of the Soviet Union.

Around two-thirds of Russia's electricity is produced by coal-, oil-, and gas-fired power plants.

ENERGY SOURCES

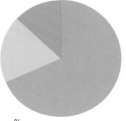

%

68.5 Oil, gas, coal, and diesel

18.7 Hydroelectricity

12.8 Nuclear

Source: Government of Russia

MAJOR INDUSTRIES

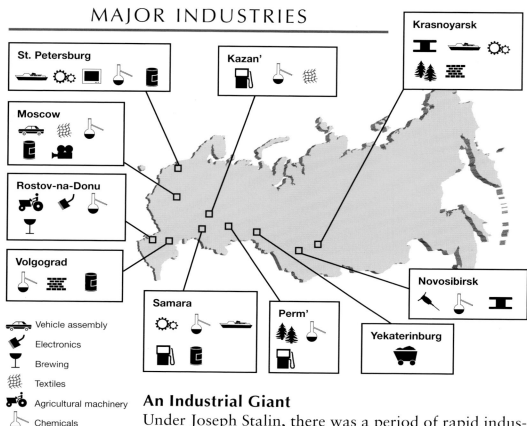

The chart above shows Russia's most important industrial centers.

An Industrial Giant

Under Joseph Stalin, there was a period of rapid industrialization in the Soviet Union. Many new mines, steelworks, and factories were built to cater to the increase in heavy industry. In 1913, Russia accounted for just 4 percent of the world's industrial output, but this rose to 10 percent in 1941 and to 20 percent by the mid-1980s. Russia became an industrial giant.

The lack of competition between businesses meant that Russia was inefficient and poor at developing new products and technologies. Since 1991, the government has sold about 75 percent of Russian industry into private hands. Nevertheless, production has dropped sharply.

Russia's rich reserves of oil and gas provide materials for the country's large chemical industries, producing fertilizers, plastics, synthetic resins, and petrochemicals. Chemical plants are concentrated in the oil- and gas-producing areas of the Volga–Ural region.

Heavy engineering, such as machine and shipbuilding, is centered in European Russia, where there is a ready supply of skilled labor. Engineering plants rely on Russia's iron and steel industry for raw materials. Textile and paper production are also important. Many of Russia's clothing factories are situated in the Caucasus, close to the cotton plantations of Central Asian countries. Russia also manufactures many luxury goods, such as watches, televisions, automobiles, refrigerators, and cameras, while its vodka (*see* p. 109) is famous throughout the world.

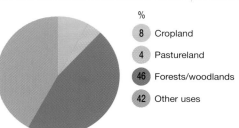

LAND USE

%
8 Cropland
4 Pastureland
46 Forests/woodlands
42 Other uses

Source: Government of Russia

Wheatfields and Forests

During the Soviet period, the government controlled all farming activity through a system of *kolkhozy* ("collective farms") and *sovkhozy* ("state farms"). Collective farms were created by forcing hundreds of thousands of peasants and small farmers to pool their land, animals, and equipment to form a larger farm. Each *kolkhoz* had

Most of Russia's vast territory cannot be used for agriculture. Almost half of the country is covered by forest, and only about 12 percent is farmland. The agricultural heartlands of Russia are the wheatfields of the Don and Volga plains.

HOW RUSSIA USES ITS LAND

Cropland
Forest
Pasture
Tundra

Women work in a field on a sovkhoz, or state farm. Today, most state farms are being sold to private business or are being divided among the people who work them.

In 1991, there were 25,800 collective farms and 21,000 state farms. By 1995, there were only 6,000 collectives and 3,600 state farms, but 17,300 commercial farms had been created.

to deliver a quota of farm goods to the government each year. This caused hardship and resentment because the quotas were often impossible to achieve.

State farms were much larger and were owned and managed directly by the government. They often concentrated on producing a single crop. Government pressure to increase production led to poor farming methods. Chemicals, fertilizers, and heavy machinery were overused. The soil was forced to produce crops quickly one after another. Over the years, these methods damaged the soil and caused serious pollution, leading to a large fall in the quantities of farm products grown.

After the breakup of the Soviet Union in 1991, private ownership of land was made legal, and many farms were taken over by individuals or businesses. Farmers are still struggling to cope with the problems of inefficiency, pollution, and over-worked soils left by the Soviet system.

Russia's farmland is found mainly in the southwest of the country. The farther east one goes, the less land there is that is suitable for crops. In the Russian Far East, only one percent is cropland. The main crops grown in Russia are grains, such as wheat, oats, rye, barley, and corn, but potatoes, sugar beet, vegetables, sunflowers, fruit, and berries are also common. Livestock farms raise beef and dairy cattle, sheep, pigs, and horses.

Not surprisingly, in a country that contains the world's biggest forest, timber makes a major contribution to the Russian economy. In 1995, Russia's forests produced a total of 4.1 million cubic feet (115 million cu. m) of timber. This was mostly softwoods such as pine or spruce.

> **In 1997, Russia was the fifth-largest producer of wheat in the world.**

Fishing Offshore and Inland

With its long Pacific and Atlantic coastlines, Russia has an important fishing industry. The total catch of the Russian fishing fleet in 1995 was 3.8 million tons. Trawlers fish the seas around Russia's coast in the Kara and Barents seas in the northwest and in the Okhotsk, Bering, Japan, and Chukchi seas in the east.

Russian factory ships roam the world's oceans processing and freezing fish, sometimes for the fishing fleets of other nations. Russia's many lakes and rivers also provide a rich harvest of salmon and trout.

Sturgeon and Caviar

The Black and Caspian seas and the rivers that flow into them—especially the Volga—are home to Russia's most famous fish, the sturgeon. The eggs, or roe, of the sturgeon are known as caviar, a special and very expensive delicacy. There are several species of sturgeon. The largest is the *beluga*, which can reach a length of 28 feet (8.5 m) and weigh more than a ton. The most expensive caviar comes from the smaller *sevruga*, which produces a black roe, and the *sterlet*, which has a golden roe.

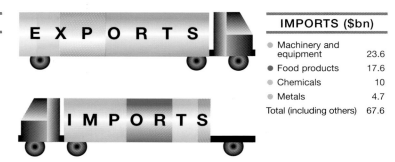

EXPORTS ($bn)	
Fuels and energy	41.4
Metals	18.2
Machinery and equipment	8.8
Chemicals	7.2
Total (including others)	87.4

Source: Government of Russia, 1997

IMPORTS ($bn)	
Machinery and equipment	23.6
Food products	17.6
Chemicals	10
Metals	4.7
Total (including others)	67.6

Russia's main exports are minerals, metals, fuels, machinery, and forestry products. The country's biggest imports are machinery, transportation equipment, foodstuffs, and chemical products.

TRADE AND TRADING PARTNERS

The Soviet Union traded mostly with other communist East European countries, such as Hungary and Poland. Russia itself, as a republic within the USSR, exchanged a variety of commodities with other Soviet republics, such as Armenia and Georgia. It sold oil and gas to republics with few energy resources and bought products it needed, such as cotton and grain. Because all the republics were part of the Soviet Union, these exchanges were not technically importing and exporting.

The CIS Trade Bloc

With the breakup of the USSR in 1991, Russia continued trading with the republics, which were now independent countries. Most of the former Soviet republics formed the Commonwealth of Independent States (CIS)—a loose economic and military association, or bloc. The only republics not to join were Latvia, Lithuania, and Estonia.

Today, Russia's main trading partners are other countries from the CIS (especially Ukraine and Belarus), Germany, the United States, and the Netherlands. Trade with nearby Turkey and Syria is also increasing. On the other hand, trade with Russia's former Eastern European allies has declined.

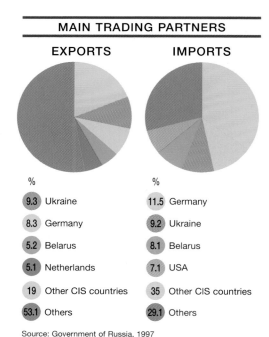

MAIN TRADING PARTNERS

EXPORTS — %: 9.3 Ukraine, 8.3 Germany, 5.2 Belarus, 5.1 Netherlands, 19 Other CIS countries, 53.1 Others

IMPORTS — %: 11.5 Germany, 9.2 Ukraine, 8.1 Belarus, 7.1 USA, 35 Other CIS countries, 29.1 Others

Source: Government of Russia, 1997

TRANSPORTATION

Transportation is very important in a country as vast as Russia, where three-quarters of the population live west of the Urals but most natural resources lie to the east. The first important links were built in the 19th century, when a massive railroad-building program was begun.

From St. Petersburg to Vladivostok

The railroad network is the most important part of the country's transportation system. The first line in Russia was built in 1837 from St. Petersburg to the czar's palace at Tsarskoye Selo—a distance of just 14 miles (22 km). Today, Russia has 96,250 miles (154,000 km) of railroads, but only just over half is used for transporting passengers. The rest serves industrial areas, especially the lines to the oil and gas fields in northwestern Siberia

All intercity trains in Russia run according to Moscow time. Stations all over Russia have clocks and timetables set accordingly.

TRANSPORTATION

Russia's road and railroad networks are concentrated west of the Ural Mountains, with their focus the Russian capital, Moscow. The difficult terrain in Siberia—especially the vast areas of swamp and permafrost—present serious problems for highway construction (see p. 32).

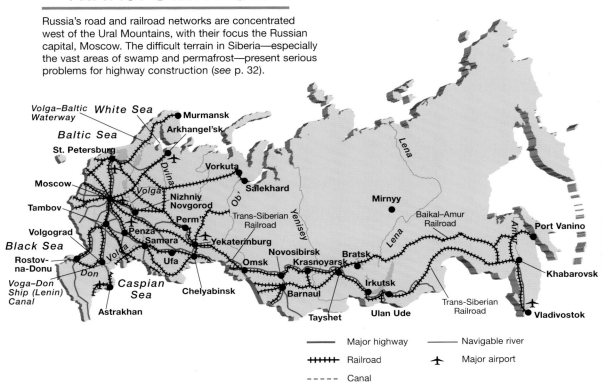

—— Major highway	—— Navigable river
┼┼┼┼┼ Railroad	✈ Major airport
- - - - Canal	

The Trans-Siberian Railroad

Every other day a train called the *Rossia* ("Russia") departs from Moscow's Yaroslavl Station and arrives in Vladivostok on the Pacific coast six-and-a-half days later, having traveled 5,786 miles (9,311 km) along the Trans-Siberian Railroad—the longest railroad in the world.

The building of the railroad started in 1891. Laborers toiled on six different sections of the route at the same time. By 1898, they had completed the line from Moscow as far as Lake Baikal. The final stretch, from Baikal via Khabarovsk to Vladivostok, was completed in 1916.

The Trans-Siberian Railroad originally carried soldiers and settlers to Siberia and East Asia, brought back tea and silk from China, and allowed Siberia to export produce to western Russia and Europe. After the October Revolution, freight trains brought food and consumer goods to the Siberian cities and returned with steel, aluminum, and timber, helping with the area's development.

The line continues to play a vital part in Russia's economy—there is still no continuous highway across Siberia. The trip is also popular with tourists.

and to the mining center of Vorkuta in the northern Urals. A quarter of Russian railroad routes have been electrified; the rest of the trains are powered by diesel locomotives.

The road network is not as well developed as railroads. Private automobiles are too expensive for most Russians, and the majority of commercial freight is carried by train. Russia has only 593,000 miles (949,000 km) of highway, compared to 3,880,000 miles (6,208,000 km) in the United States, a country almost half the size.

Many of the mining settlements in central and northern Siberia are supplied by ships using the Ob', Yenisey, and Lena rivers. River transportation is difficult and unreliable because the rivers are iced over for up to eight months of the year, and water levels can be low in summer.

By Water, By Air

Water transportation is important in western Russia too, where river systems and lakes are linked by canals. In 1952, the government of the Soviet Union completed the Lenin Ship Canal, connecting European Russia's longest

MAIN FOREIGN ARRIVALS

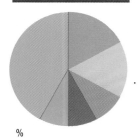

%

17 China

16 Finland

9 Germany

8 Poland

8 Mongolia

42 Others

Source: Government of Russia

Passengers wait in the snow to board a train at Klin, a town on the St. Petersburg–Moscow railroad. Trains are cheap and reliable. For long journeys, passengers can rent spacious and comfortable sleepers.

rivers—the Don and the Volga. Ships can sail between the Black, Caspian, Baltic, and White seas, and between the ports of Rostov, Astrakhan, Volgograd, Moscow, Samara, St. Petersburg, and Arkhangel'sk.

Air travel is the fastest way to cover the huge distances between Russia's cities, especially in Siberia. Some remote settlements in Siberia are only accessible by air. The former Soviet airline, *Aeroflot* ("Airfleet"), has been split into hundreds of smaller airlines, many of them with little money and poor maintenance records. As a result, air travel in Russia can be unreliable and occasionally unsafe.

The First Nuclear-Powered Ship

The world's first nuclear-powered ship, the *Lenin*, was built in Leningrad (St. Petersburg) in 1957. The ship was named after the first communist leader of Russia. An icebreaker, the *Lenin* once plowed through the thick ice that sometimes blocks Russia's Baltic and Arctic ports in winter, freeing them for use by shipping. The *Lenin* was powered by three nuclear reactors, enabling it to travel huge distances and through severe weather conditions without having to refuel. Toward the end of the Soviet era, the Russian navy dumped the *Lenin*'s three damaged reactors into the Barents Sea.

Arts and Living

"The houses are built with wood of fir trees, joined one with another…without any iron or stone work, covered with birch branches. …Their churches are all of wood…"

An English merchant visiting Russia in 1557

Many of the customs and traditions that we today think of as being distinctively "Russian" are rooted in the Slavic culture of medieval Rus'. Folk dances, such as the stamping dance; elaborate crafts, such as the beautiful enameled boxes called *palekh*, and wood carving and glass making all stem from this time. The most powerful influence, though, was the Russian Orthodox church. Its rites and observances marked the passing of people's lives, while its churches and icons, or sacred images, were the dominant forms of architecture and art.

From the 17th century, Russian culture increasingly took its inspiration from Europe. By the 19th century, aristocrats were as likely to speak French as Russian. Many of the architects and painters who worked for the Russian czars came from Italy, France, or Germany. New forms of art were introduced, including portraits and paintings of famous events. In the 19th century, Russian writers wrote the first great Russian novels.

In the 20th century, the Soviet regime rebuilt Russia as a socialist country. It tried to direct the way people lived; it banned many books, pictures, and movies; and took away the power of the church. Nevertheless, a secret, "underground" culture flourished: Banned books were circulated in secret editions, and people gathered in private to discuss art and politics. Since the fall of the USSR, there are signs of a revival in Russia's rich folk traditions.

Matryoshka, or "Russian," dolls are the most famous kind of woodcraft found in Russia. Inside the matryoshka is a succession of smaller dolls.

FACT FILE

● Russia uses the Cyrillic alphabet. Some of its letters look the same as those used in our Roman one but in fact represent different sounds. The capital letter "P" for example, is roughly equivalent to the Roman "R."

● At the time of the 1917 Revolution, there were more than 50,000 Orthodox churches in Russia. By 1988, there were just 7,000. Five years later, after the fall of the USSR, there were some 20,000.

● Poet Osip Mandelstam (1891–1938) died in a Siberian Gulag after he was arrested for writing a poem that criticized Soviet leader Joseph Stalin.

97

ARTS

Russia's long winter nights enabled its peoples to create a rich tradition of arts, crafts, and storytelling. Over the centuries, both the church and government had a powerful influence in shaping these traditions.

This icon, or sacred image, shows the Virgin Hodegetria ("Mother of God"). Traditionally, it was believed that the first icons were made in Heaven and had miraculous (wonder-working) powers. Because of their supposed divine origins, new icons were usually copies of old ones.

From Icons to Posters

Until the 18th century, most Russian art took the form of icons—religious paintings of Jesus Christ, the Virgin Mary, and the saints that were usually painted on small wooden panels. The word *icon* comes from the Greek word *eikon*, meaning simply "image." Icons were usually displayed in Russian Orthodox churches on a large wooden screen called an iconostasis (*see* p. 102). Sometimes, though, people carried them through the streets in religious processions or kept them at home to inspire them with their prayers.

One of the best icon artists was the monk Andrey Rublev (about 1360–1430). His most famous work is the *Old Testament Trinity*, which shows God the Father, the Son, and the Holy Ghost as guests of Abraham, the Old Testament patriarch. The icon is now on display in Moscow's Tretyakov Gallery.

Russian art was given a fresh direction in the 19th century by a group of painters called the *Peredvizhniki* ("The Wanderers"). They painted pictures of ordinary people and historic events, as well as portraits of famous figures. The best-known of the Wanderers is Ilya Repin (1844–1930), who was trained by a provincial icon painter. One of his most famous and popular works, the horrific *Ivan the Terrible with the Body of his Son*, shows the terrified czar cradling the head of his son, whom he has just murdered in a fit of rage.

Fabergé Eggs

Peter Carl Fabergé (1846–1920) was the court jeweler and goldsmith to Russia's last two czars, Alexander III and Nicholas II. His elaborate, luxurious designs for household items such as picture frames, clocks, and cigarette cases became known all over the world. Fabergé, who was originally based in St. Petersburg, was able to set up workshops in Kiev, Moscow, Odessa, and London. Fabergé's most famous objects were the beautiful gilded and jeweled Easter eggs he made for the Romanovs. After the Bolsheviks came to power in 1917, they took over the Fabergé company, and the jeweler fled abroad.

Just before the Russian Revolution, talented painters such as Kazimir Malevich (1878–1935) developed a kind of abstract art called Suprematism. Malevich did not want to portray the real world but created dynamic arrangements of geometric shapes. The Suprematists wanted an art that was in tune with the revolutionary times.

At first, the new Soviet regime welcomed the new art. The government commissioned many of the new artists to make ceramics and posters commemorating the revolution. Early in the 1920s, however, the Communist Party decreed that all art had to project a positive view of Soviet life. Many artists chose to go into exile, among them Marc Chagall (1887–1985). Chagall, who was at first enthusiastic about the revolution and who became a government official in charge of the arts, soon found his wistful, fantastic images of peasant life got him into trouble, and he left to live in Paris.

The new Soviet art showed images of heroic workers, joyful peasants, and inspiring leaders in a style called Socialist Realism. More than two million statues of Lenin and Stalin were put up in towns and cities all over the USSR.

Many of the artists who created the revolutionary painting of the early 20th century were women. One of these was Liubov Popova (1889–1924), who painted this energetic and colorful picture below.

A Russian Fairy Tale

The Russians have a rich tradition of telling folk stories and fairy tales. One of the most loved is the story of Snyegurochka, or the Snow Maiden. The tale goes like this. Once upon a time, there was an old man and his wife who had everything they wanted except for a child. One snowy day in winter, as they sat in their *izba*, or wooden house, they decided to build themselves a daughter out of snow. They gave her eyes made out of deep-blue beads, and a piece of red ribbon for her mouth. Suddenly, to the old couple's joy, the beautiful snow maiden smiled. They took her into their house and looked after her as their own daughter, calling her Snyegurochka. Spring came, but Snyegurochka grew sadder and sadder and refused to go out into the sunshine. Finally, in summer, the snow maiden's friends persuaded her to go berrying in the woods. They decided to build a bonfire to celebrate summer, and jumped over it. "Jump, jump, Snyegurochka!" the girls cried. She jumped and vanished in a wisp of steam.

With the return of religious freedom after the fall of the Soviet Union, and the rebuilding of many cathedrals and churches, there has been a revival of icon painting. One of the most popular artists in Russia today is Ilya Glazunov (born 1930).

A Great Literature

Russian literature first flourished in the 19th century. Aleksandr Pushkin (1799–1837; *see* box opposite) is Russia's favorite poet and considered by many people to be the father of Russian literature. Children learn his poetry at school, and many Russians can still recite it by heart when they are adults. Pushkin's most famous works are his novel in verse, *Yevgeny Onegin*, a tragic tale of love and honor, and *Boris Godunov*, a tragic play about one of Russia's most famous rulers. Like his hero Onegin, Pushkin died fighting a duel to defend his wife's reputation.

Fyodor Dostoyevsky (1821–1881) is one of the world's greatest novelists. His best works—*Crime and Punishment* and *The Brothers Karamazov*—are dark, psychological tales that exposed the corruption, poverty, and despair that lurked in Russian society. Novelist Lev Tolstoy (1828–1910), by contrast, portrayed the brilliant life of the Russian aristocracy. Probably the most famous Russian novel of the 19th century is Tolstoy's *War and Peace*. It is a sweeping epic set during the Napoleonic Wars, when Russia was invaded by the French.

Anton Chekhov (1860–1904) was a master at writing short stories, but he is best known for his plays. *The Cherry Orchard*,

A Poem by Pushkin

Aleksandr Pushkin (below) wrote this poem, "The Flower," after finding a dried flower pressed in a book in 1828.

A flower—shrivelled, lacking fragrance,
Forgotten on a page—I see,
And instantly my soul awakens,
Filled with the strangest reverie:

When did it bloom? Last spring?
Earlier?
How long? Where was it plucked?
By whom?
By foreign hands? Familiar?
And why put here, as in a tomb?

To mark a tender meeting by it?
A parting with a precious one?
Or just a walk—alone and quiet—
In forests' shade? In meadows' sun?

Is she alive? Is he still with her?
Where is their haven at this hour?
Or did they both already wither,
Like this unfathomable flower?

Uncle Vanya, and *The Seagull* are still regularly performed in theaters around the world. The characters of his plays are often members of the landed gentry who live on decrepit country estates miles from Moscow. Billed as comedies, the plays are nevertheless full of melancholy and the sense that the old Russia is disappearing.

The Soviet regime persecuted many of Russia's best 20th-century writers. Boris Pasternak (1890–1960) was a poet and novelist. His novel *Dr. Zhivago* won the Nobel Prize in Literature in 1958. It was first published in the West in translation, and only appeared in Russian years later. The Soviet authorities forced Pasternak to refuse the Nobel award, and his books were banned.

There have been four Russian winners of the Nobel Prize in Literature:
- **Ivan Bunin (1935)**
- **Boris Pasternak (1958)**
- **Mikhail Sholokhov (1965)**
- **Alexander Solzhenitsyn (1970)**

Novelist Alexander Solzhenitsyn (born 1918) vividly described the horrors of life in a Gulag labor camp in *One Day in the Life of Ivan Denisovich* and *The Gulag Archipelago* and was banished from the Soviet Union. He lived in the United States for 20 years before returning to Russia in 1994.

Music and Dance

Russia has given us some of the world's finest classical music. Nineteenth-century composers such as Mikhail Glinka (1804–1857), who wrote Russia's national anthem, drew their inspiration from traditional Slavic folk music and dances. Modest Mussorgsky (1839–1881) created a brilliant opera from Pushkin's classic tale, *Boris Godunov*, and composed the piano suite *Pictures from an Exhibition*. Russian fairy tales provided the basis for the operas of Nikolai Rimsky-Korsakov (1844–1908), from which comes the famous "Flight of the Bumblebee."

Perhaps the best known Russian composer is Pyotr Tchaikovsky (1840–1893), whose ballets *Swan Lake*, *The Sleeping Beauty*, and *The Nutcracker Suite* are loved all over the world. He also wrote six symphonies, eleven operas, and the magnificent *1812 Overture*, in which crashing guns recall the battle with Napoleon's army at Borodino outside Moscow in 1812.

The 20th century produced the Romantic composer Sergey Rachmaninoff (1873–1943), and Sergey Prokofiev (1891–1953), who wrote the music for the ballet

A Ballets Russes theater program depicts the great Russian dancer Vaslav Nijinsky in his role as the faun in the ballet L'Après-midi d'un faune ("Afternoon of a Faun"). Nijinsky made his debut as a dancer in the Mariinsky Theater in St. Petersburg.

Romeo and Juliet and created *Peter and the Wolf*, a children's favorite. Igor Stravinsky (1882–1971) broke with traditional classical music. The intense rhythms and disharmonies of his compositions shocked audiences when they were first performed. He composed ballets for the famous Ballets Russes dance company, including the exhilarating *The Rite of Spring*.

Russia's most famous ballet companies are the Mariinsky Ballet (formerly the Kirov) in St. Petersburg and the Bolshoi Ballet in Moscow, both of which were founded in the 18th century. Anna Pavlova (1881–1931) and Vaslav Nijinsky (1890–1950), the two leading dancers of the early 20th century, both trained with the Mariinsky before joining the Ballets Russes ("Russian Ballets"). Many of the best dancers of the Soviet period—Rudolf Nureyev (1938–1993), Natalia Makarova (born 1940), and Mikhail Baryshnikov (born 1948)—left for the West and the higher rates of pay they could demand there.

Traditional folk music choirs and dance ensembles are popular among Russians. Songs are often accompanied by an accordion and a *balalaika*, an instrument something like a guitar but with a triangular body and three strings.

The motion-picture director Sergey Eisenstein's final epic movie, made in two parts in 1944 and 1946, told the story of the Russian czar Ivan the Terrible. Contemporary Russian moviegoers could hardly have failed to spot the relevance of Ivan's fearsome reign to the rule of the Soviet leader Stalin.

At the Movies

Going to the movies is very popular in Russia. There is a long tradition of film-making—the first Russian movie appeared in 1907. Moscow is the main center for movie-making. During the Soviet period, most movies had historical themes or they glorified Soviet achievements. *The Battleship Potemkin* (1925), directed by Sergey Eisenstein, tells the story of a mutiny by sailors during the 1905 St. Petersburg rising. Many critics still regard it as one of the finest movies ever made, with its revolutionary use of montage—the putting together of a succession of different shots.

In Soviet Russia, all movies were censored (checked for their content), and many were banned. Nevertheless, some directors were still able to make very fine movies. Andrey Tarkovsky (1932–1986) worked for the Mosfilm Studios in Moscow and made such poetic masterpieces as *Andrey Rublyov* (1966) and *The Sacrifice* (1986).

After the fall of the Soviet Union, there were signs of a revival in Russian cinema. Many once-banned films were shown for the first time in Russia.

Log Cabins, Onion Domes, and "Seven Sisters"

In Russia, there is far more timber than stone, and until the 18th century, many buildings were made out of wood. The traditional, one-story *izba*—a simple log cabin with a thatched roof—can still be seen in old Russian villages.

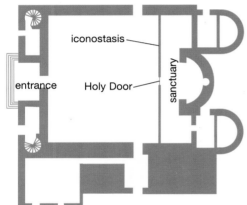

iconostasis

entrance Holy Door

sanctuary

In a typical Russian Orthodox church, the iconostasis, or icon stand, divides the main body of the church from the sanctuary, or altar area. Only the priest is allowed in the sanctuary, which he leaves and enters through the Holy Door.

When Russia adopted Orthodox Christianity from Constantinople, it also copied the Byzantine style of church building. This design used a simple square plan and a central dome. By the 13th century, this style was adapted for building in wood, with steeper gables and onion-shaped domes added to throw off the heavy snows of winter.

The churches built in Moscow in the 15th and 16th centuries copied the shapes of the old wooden churches, creating a distinctive Russian style of church architecture. This can be seen in the Kremlin cathedrals (1475–1510; *see* p. 37) and St. Basil's Cathedral (1555–1560; *see* pp. 6 and 37) in Red Square, Moscow. St. Basil's, with its cluster of polychromatic (many-colored) towers and turban-shaped domes, looks like a fairy-tale palace.

The interiors of Russian churches are richly decorated with wall paintings, icons, and mosaics. The iconostasis, which divides the altar from the main body of the church, is hung with six tiers of icons, arranged in a special order.

Stalinist Architecture

As part of Stalin's campaign to modernize and industrialize Russia, he began a massive building program. At the center of Stalin's plans was the reconstruction of Moscow as a "truly Socialist city." New boulevards were driven through the city center, and the extraordinary Metro stations built (see pp. 38–39). Old buildings were torn down, and gigantic new ones were put up. Stalin wanted the new buildings, which included the Military Academy, the Red Army Theater, and the People's Commissariat for Defense, to express the might and heroism of Soviet Russia. The buildings were majestic, simple, and bold and looked back to the architecture of ancient Greece. "Stalinist" architecture reached its height in the seven elaborately decorated skyscrapers built in Moscow in the early 1950s (below). Towering over the city's skyline, they are known as the "Seven Sisters."

When Peter the Great built his new capital at St. Petersburg, he decided to break with tradition. He invited foreign architects to design the buildings and sent young Russians to study in the West. The most famous of St. Petersburg's architects was the Italian Bartolomeo Rastrelli (1700–1771), who created the magnificent Winter Palace (1754–1762; see p. 44) in the elaborate Italian style known as Baroque.

At the beginning of the 20th century, architects built exciting new buildings made of glass and concrete. Under the Soviet regime, Joseph Stalin encouraged the construction of huge, awe-inspiring buildings (see box). Today, the Russian government concentrates on restoring and preserving some of the country's old churches and monasteries.

DAILY LIFE

The standard of living in Russia is far below that enjoyed by most people in the United States. The Russian people, however, are resilient and resourceful and manage to make the best of what little they have.

Food and Drink

Traditional Russian cooking is based on hearty peasant food. Meat, fish, potatoes, and cabbage are the main ingredients. Classic Russian dishes include *borscht*, a beet and cabbage soup; *okroshka*, a chilled summer soup made with cucumber, onion, hard-boiled egg, and *kvas* (a weak beer made from fermented rye bread); and beef Stroganoff, which is thin strips of braised beef in a sauce of sour cream, onion, and wild mushrooms.

Russians are friendly and hospitable. For a visitor to a Russian home, dinner usually begins with a spread of appetizers, called *zakuski*. These include smoked fish,

Despite their country's troubles, Russians love to get together in each other's homes to eat, drink, and chat. Here, some friends celebrate a birthday in a Moscow apartment.

Blini

These plump, little pancakes are made using buckwheat—made from an earthy, kind of flour that is popular in Russia. Ask an adult to help you with frying the pancakes, as this can be difficult.

You will need:

3 oz (75g) buckwheat flour, 1 tbls sugar, 1/2 tsp salt, 1 1/2 oz dried yeast, 1/2 oz (15g) butter, 1/2 pt (275ml) milk, 3 oz (75g) plain flour, 2 egg yolks, 5 fl oz sour cream, 1 egg white, some oil

Method:

Mix the flour, sugar, salt, and yeast in a large warmed bowl. Melt the butter in a small pan with half the milk, and then beat into the yeast mixture. Cover the bowl with a dish towel and leave to stand in a warm place until the mixture has doubled in volume. Heat the remainder of the milk until it is lukewarm, and then stir it into the batter with the plain flour, egg yolks, and sour cream and beat for 1 minute. Cover and leave for another hour. Whisk the egg white until stiff and fold carefully into the batter. Pour the batter into a jug.

Place a griddle over a medium heat and brush with oil. Pour a little batter into the griddle to form a small circle. Add 3 or 4 more batter circles, and cook for 1 minute. Turn the pancakes over and cook for another 30 seconds until golden brown. Repeat until all the batter has been used, keeping the cooked pancakes warm in a heated oven. Serve the pancakes warm, spread with butter and topped with chopped egg or smoked salmon.

salads, salami, mushrooms baked in sour cream, *blini* (small pancakes; *see* box), and caviar. Caviar, called *ikra* in Russian, is the roe of the sturgeon (*see* p. 91). The salty fish eggs are eaten chilled, with *blini* or buttered toast and a squirt of lemon juice. *Zakuski* are eaten with dark rye bread.

Pickles are often served with food. Pickling vegetables in vinegar is a useful way of preserving them during the long winter. People like to eat sweet and sour gherkins, and pickled mushrooms, beets, or garlic.

How to Say...

Russian is overwhelmingly the most common language spoken in the Russian Federation. Even people for whom Russian is not their mother tongue are usually able to speak the language. Russian is a Slavic language, related to other languages spoken in eastern Europe, such as Serbian, Ukrainian, Bulgarian, and Slovene.

The Russian language uses a different alphabet from the Roman alphabet used by many Western languages, such as English and French. In the ninth century, two Greek missionary brothers, Saint Cyril and Saint Methodius, developed a new alphabet in order to translate the Bible from Greek into Slavonic—a Slavic language related to modern Russian. The brothers, who were skillful linguists, adapted 43 letters from the Greek and Hebrew alphabets to represent the rich variety of sounds in Slavonic. The alphabet was called Cyrillic after one of the brothers. Versions of the Cyrillic alphabet are used by most modern Slavic languages, including Russian, Ukrainian, Serbian, and Bulgarian. The modern Russian alphabet has 32 letters.

Russian is not an easy language to learn, but it is a very beautiful one. Here are some useful phrases in transliterated Russian. The Russian phrase is followed by the way to pronounce it. The capital letters show where the stress falls in the phrase.

Yes *Da* (dah) No *Net* (nyet)

Hello *Zdrastvuitye* (ZDRAST-voot-yeh)

Good morning *Dobroye utro*
 (DOH-bra-yuh OOT-rah)

Good evening *Dobriy vecher*
 (DOH-bri VYEH-chur)

Goodbye *Do svidaniya*
 (das-vi-DAN-yah)

Please/You're welcome
 Pozhaluista (pah-ZHAL-oo-sta)

Thank you *Spasiba* (spa-SEE-bah)

How are you? *Kak dela?* (kak dyi-LAH)

Fine, thank you *Khorosho*
 (kha-ra-SHO)

What's your name? *Kak vas zovut?*
 (kak vas za-VOOT)

My name is... Myenya zovut...
 (min-YAH za-VOOT...)

I don't understand *Ya nye ponimayu*
 (yah ne pah-nee-MA-yoo)

Where are you from? *Otkuda vy?*
 (at-KOO-dah vi)

America *Amerika* (uh-MYEH-ri-kuh)

I want... *Ya khochu...* (ya kha-CHOO)

Numbers:

One *Odyin* (ah-DYIN)

Two *Dva* (dva)

Three *Tre* (tree)

Four *Chetiryeh* (chi-TIR-yeh)

Five *Pyaht* (pyaht)

Six *Shest* (shest)

Seven *Syem* (syem)

Eight *Vosyim* (VO-syim)

Nine *Dyevyut* (DYEV-yut)

Ten *Dyesyut* (DYES-yut)

Russians also love to eat pies. *Pirozkhi* are small pies containing cabbage, carrot, rice, and ground beef. These pies are often served with *borscht*.

Russia's most popular non-alcoholic drink is tea. This is traditionally made with a *samovar*, a water urn heated by a central tube filled with burning charcoal or pine cones. The tea leaves are first infused in a small teapot, which is kept warm on top of the *samovar*. Then the highly concentrated brew is diluted with hot water from the urn. Tea is served in glasses rather than cups and is drunk with lemon and sugar.

Vodka

The first ruler of Rus', Vladimir, is reputed to have said: "Drinking is the joy of Rus'. We cannot live without it." Today, Russia's most popular alcoholic drink is vodka—a colorless spirit made from wheat or rye. Its name comes from the Russian for "water." During the long winter months, Russians like to serve it in small glasses to accompany caviar or salmon. Often it is flavored with herbs or lemon, or colored red with paprika. Today, many people are worried by the rise of alcoholism in Russia. The average Russian drinks a bottle of vodka a week.

Education

The Soviet government kept a tight grip on education. Children had to learn the basics of Marxist beliefs. Subjects, particularly history, were taught in such a way as to glorify communism and the Russian nation. Books used in classrooms were carefully censored because the government wanted to educate loyal Soviet citizens.

Today, the government of the Russian Federation continues to control education, but Marxist ideas are no longer taught. New, uncensored books have been introduced, and the curriculum has been revised to reflect a diversity of ideas. Both teachers and pupils are able to express their opinions freely.

Many Russian children attend preschool, but compulsory education begins at age seven and continues to age fifteen. More than half of Russian children stay in school for longer—up to the age of 17. In the non-Russian republics of the federation, children are usually taught in their own languages, but they also have to learn Russian.

EDUCATIONAL ATTENDANCE

University and college	13.9%
Secondary	54.5%
Primary	89.5%

Public Holidays

January 1	New Year's Day
January 7	Russian Orthodox Christmas Day
February 23	Defenders of the Motherland Day (anniversary of the founding of the Red Army)
March 8	International Women's Day
May 1 and 2	International Labor Day and Spring Festival
May 9	Victory Day (anniversary of the end of World War II in 1945)
June 12	Russian Independence Day
November 7	Anniversary of the Great October Socialist Revolution

Russian pupils have to work very hard to get into one of their country's universities. In today's Russia, universities do not have much money, and there are few places available. Students study for five years before taking their first degree. The most famous of Russia's universities are found in the capital city, Moscow, and in St. Petersburg.

Holidays and Festivals

The most important festivals in the Russian year are Christmas and Easter. These have different dates than in the West because the Russian Orthodox church still uses the Julian calendar (*see* p. 58). Christmas Day, for example, falls on January 7.

Easter Day, called *paskha* in Russian, begins with a midnight church service. At dawn, the Lenten fast is broken with specially made cakes and puddings. A cake made of curd cheese, sugar, sour cream, candied fruit, and nuts is pressed into a wooden, pyramid-shaped mold. The top of the cake is decorated with candied fruit in the form of the letters "X" and "B." In the Cyrillic alphabet, these letters stand for *Khristos Voskress*, meaning "Christ is risen." There is also a tradition of decorating Easter eggs. Some are boiled with onion skins to give the shell a yellow color, then painted with festive or religious scenes.

The New Year is celebrated in the same way that Christmas is in the West. Presents are exchanged around a festive fir tree called a *yolka*. Instead of Santa Claus, there is old Grandfather Frost.

The Soviet festivals of International Labor Day and November 7—the anniversary of the "Great October Socialist Revolution"—are still public holidays. During the Soviet period, these festivals were marked by huge military parades in Moscow's Red Square.

Sports and Pastimes

The most popular spectator sports in Russia are soccer (*futbol*), ice hockey (*khokkey*), and basketball (*basketbol*). Horse racing is also very popular, and in winter, *troyka* racing takes place in local hippodromes. A *troyka* is a traditional vehicle drawn by three horses.

Russia is one of the most successful sporting nations in the world. From 1896 to 1998, it won 572 gold medals in the summer and winter Olympic Games. The Russian national ice-hockey team won the silver medal at the 1998 Winter Olympics. Moscow's top soccer teams—Spartak and Dinamo—compete regularly in international events.

In such a wintry climate, it is not surprising that skating and cross-country skiing are favorite winter pastimes for Russians. In many towns and cities, ponds in public parks are allowed to freeze over to provide outdoor skating rinks. In summer, swimming, walking, and fishing trips are popular outdoor pursuits. On weekends, many Russians go to a *dacha*, a wooden cottage in the countryside, where they can escape from the bustle of city life.

Mushroom-hunting is almost a national sport, and everyone has a favorite "secret" spot in the forest where the best mushrooms grow. The delicious wild mushrooms are dried or pickled and are used to add flavor to stews.

Russia has produced some of the world's finest gymnasts. This Russian girl is competing in the rhythmic exercise that is part of gymnastic competitions.

Nights at the Circus

The circus is very popular in Russia. Adults and children alike love to spend an afternoon or evening under a "big top." Russian circus is a very traditional show, with dance and music, followed by acrobats, tightrope walkers, jugglers, performing animals, and clowns.

Circus was first developed in England in the 18th century. A showman named Philip Astley put on a performance involving trick horseback riding and music. Later, he added acrobats and clowns. He staged his shows in a circular building called a circus—the word *circus* comes from the Latin for "circle."

The Russian empress Catherine the Great invited the English trick rider Charles Hughes to set up a riding school in St. Petersburg. Hughes made circus popular in Russia, and eventually there were families of performers—including the Durovs, Zapashnys, Kios, and Kantemirovs—who passed on their skills from one generation to the next. The first permanent circus was set up in St. Petersburg in 1877.

In Soviet Russia, the government supported the circus. In the early 1990s, there were some 70 permanent circus buildings and about 50 traveling circuses. Since the end of the Soviet Union, however, many circuses have lost their financial support and their future is threatened. Still, Russia's biggest and best circus remains the world-famous Moscow Circus, with a company of some 7,000 performers. Here, clowns from the circus entertain the spectators.

Chess is also enjoyed by many Russians, who are taught how to play while still at school. Almost every world chess champion since 1949 has been a Soviet citizen. Mikhail Botvinnik held the title of world champion for 13 years.

Freeing the Media

During the Soviet period, the media were tightly controlled by the Communist Party. Newspapers, television, and radio were used for propaganda; that is, to express the government's point of view. Since 1991, Russian television and newspaper companies have been privatized, and the media are now as free as in the West.

Almost all Russian households have a television set. The main national networks are *Ostankino* and Russian Television, but many new ones are starting up. The new channels show a lot of American and European programs in addition to home-produced material. Radio has also been freed from government control—there are dozens of new FM stations broadcasting rock music, talk radio, and 24-hour news.

Russians are avid readers, and there are some 8,000 newspaper and magazine titles to choose from. The main daily newspapers are *Izvestia, Moskovsky Komsomolets,* and *Komsomolskaya Pravda. Argumenty i Fakty* ("Arguments and Facts") is a popular weekly news magazine, the Russian equivalent of *Time* or *Newsweek*. There are also two daily newspapers in English, *The Moscow Times* and *The Moscow Tribune*.

HOW THE RUSSIANS SPEND THEIR MONEY

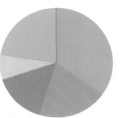

%
- 39.8 Food/drink
- 19.4 Clothing
- 8.3 Housing/household goods
- 4.6 Leisure
- 27.9 Other

Source: Government of Russia, 1994

Much of Russians' incomes goes toward meeting basic needs, such as food and housing. During the 1990s, food prices and rents increased rapidly, making it even harder for people to make ends meet.

WHAT DO THE RUSSIANS OWN?

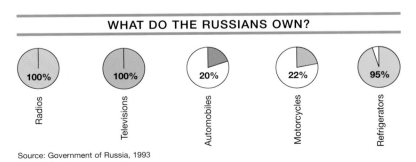

Radios 100% | Televisions 100% | Automobiles 20% | Motorcycles 22% | Refrigerators 95%

Source: Government of Russia, 1993

While most Russian homes have basic household items, such as a TV and refrigerator, only a few Russians own an automobile.

Russian Orthodoxy and Other Religions

For centuries, religion has played an important role in
Russia. In ancient times, many of the peoples living in
Russia were shamanists, worshipers of the spirits of
nature. Even today, some of the Mari and Udmurt peoples of the Volga region are shamanist. Over the
centuries, however, most peoples within the Russian
Federation have adopted Christianity, Judaism, or Islam.

People's religious beliefs are often related to the language they speak. For example, many Slavs are Orthodox Christian, while many Turkic-speaking groups are
Muslim. There are exceptions, however. The Turkic-
speaking Chuvash, for example, are mainly Christian,
while the Turkic-speaking Altai, Khakass, and Tuvans
are Buddhists. Other Buddhist followers include the
Mongolian speakers, the Buryats and Kalmucks.

Peoples' freedom to practice their faith has been
dependent on the political situation in which they lived.
Under the czars, the official religion was the Russian

*Russian Orthodox
beliefs and practices
are very traditional,
and church ceremonies
are solemn and
splendid. Orthodox
churches have no
statues, no seats, and
no instrumental music.
Only the human voice
is allowed to praise
God, and services are
accompanied by a
choir and the chanting
of the priest. Here,
bishops celebrate mass
in a Siberian monastery.*

Orthodox church, and people who practiced other religions sometimes suffered persecution. During the late 19th century, Russians carried out organized massacres of the Jews called *pogroms*. During the Soviet period, religious freedom was formally protected, but in fact many religious activities were strictly limited by the government.

Since the breakup of the USSR, there has been far more religious freedom. Many people have been attracted to various religious faiths, and nationalists—people who want a strong and traditional Russia—have reclaimed the Russian Orthodox church as an important part of Russian culture.

The Russian Orthodox church remains the primary religion in Russia. The church was founded in 988 (*see* pp. 53–54) and was independent of the Western church in Rome (later the Roman Catholic church). This came about because Orthodox (from the Greek for "right belief") leaders believed that the pope—the leader of the Western church—was straying from the original teachings of Christianity.

The seat of the Russian Orthodox church moved from Kiev to Moscow in the 14th century, where it remains today. Church leaders are called patriarchs. The head of the church has his residence at the Danilov Monastery in Moscow.

Islam is another important religion in Russia, especially among the peoples of the Caucasus and the Volga regions. Russian Muslims are not as strict as those in many countries: Women do not usually wear a veil, and the Muslim holy day—Friday— is not observed as a day of rest.

Judaism in Russia

Being Jewish in Russia is considered a nationality rather than a religion. In the 1920s and 1930s, the Soviet government set up an autonomous homeland in the Russian Far East. Some 40,000 Russian Jews journeyed to the area, although only a third stayed. The region still survives as the *oblast* of Birobidzhan, although the Jewish population now is small. Since the late 1980s, when immigration to Israel and other countries was first allowed, Russia's Jewish population has been steadily decreasing. Today, there are some 700,000 Jews in Russia, but only a few of these actually practice Judaism. There are about 30 active synagogues in Russia.

Much as some Roman Catholic churches use Latin, the Russian Orthodox church uses another "dead" language Old Church Slavonic.

The Future

"I believe, as Lenin said, that this revolutionary chaos may yet crystallize into new forms of life."

Former Soviet president Mikhail Gorbachev

Russia has come a long way since the breakup of the Soviet Union in 1991. Free elections have been held. Freedom of speech, of assembly, of movement, and of religion are all part of the 1993 Constitution. A market economy has been established; democracy has replaced dictatorship. The once drab and dirty capital, Moscow, has been transformed into a lively and cosmopolitan city. However, Russia is not yet a stable country and its future is still filled with uncertainty.

AN ECONOMY IN TURMOIL

Russia's changeover from communism to capitalism was bound to be a difficult one. However, the country has plunged far deeper into economic turmoil than anyone could have predicted. Despite the billions of dollars of aid poured into the country from international banks, the Russian currency, the ruble, has lost much of its value, and thousands of businesses have closed.

It is ordinary Russian citizens who have fared worst during the economic collapse. Often, both government and companies are too poor to be able to pay their employees. Many people have lost their jobs. Others have seen their savings wiped out because of the ruble's collapse.

Faced with such adversity, Russians have shown their customary resourcefulness. Forced to live without a salary, many Russians survive by bartering—exchanging

Teenagers celebrate the failure of the 1991 coup that attempted to reinstate the old Soviet Union. Russia's young people overwhelmingly support reform.

FACT FILE

● In the late 1990s, about one in two Russian workers received no check on payday at all.

● Russia remains a nuclear superpower, with some 22,000 warheads in its arsenal. Because many of these are located in the republics, experts are concerned about what might happen if the Russian Federation were to collapse.

● In early 2000, acting president Vladimir Putin noted that Russia would need an economic growth of 8 percent of GNP for 15 years to achieve the standard of living enjoyed by even poor European nations such as Portugal.

Chechnya

RUSSIA

NORTH OSSETIA

INGUSHETIA

CHECHNYA

GROZNY

DAGESTAN

GEORGIA

N

Chechnya is a tiny republic deep in the Caucasus. It is smaller in size than New Jersey and has a population of about one million, most of whom are Muslim.

There is a long history of conflict between Russia and Chechnya. The Russian czars conquered the Chechen homelands in the 19th century, although only after centuries of determined Chechen resistance. During the Soviet period, the Chechens and their neighbors the Ingush were given some independence as the Checheno-Ingush Autonomous Socialist Republic. However, Moscow often aggressively imposed its rule. During World War II (1939–1945), Stalin forcibly removed the entire Chechen and Ingush population because he feared that they would join with the advancing Germans.

After the Soviet Union collapsed in 1991, the Chechens declared independence and tried to break away from Russia. Fearing the break-up of the whole of the federation and the loss of valuable oil pipelines that run between Russia and the Caspian Sea, Russia invaded and a bloody war broke out in 1994. Some 80,000 people were killed before a ceasefire in 1996 established Chechnya's independence as a republic within the Russian Federation.

In 1999, Russia launched a full-scale invasion of Chechnya. It claimed that the country was harboring Islamic terrorists and guerrillas who were struggling to

win full independence for Chechnya's neighbor Dagestan. In reality, though, it seems that Russia wanted to improve on its military reputation after the failure of the 1994–1996 war, and to distract the Russian people's attention from the country's economic and social problems. The war continued into the 21st century, with atrocities and human-rights abuses committed by both sides.

Russia's conflict with the Chechen Republic reveals the difficulties hampering Russia's evolvement from a communist dictatorship to a democratic federation. Some people see the conflict as part of a far-reaching conspiracy to reimpose central rule and re-create the Soviet empire. Most people argue, though, that the crisis arose out of the chaos that reigned in a changing Russia. There was still confusion, they say, about the proper relation between a central government in Moscow and the republics. Old Soviet ways of doing things were still in place, they argue.

goods and services. Some grow their own food in small gardens outside town. Even businesses have had to barter to get through the hard times. One textile plant is said to have given the local police 6,000 pairs of socks in return for a break in paying its taxes. There are people, however, who have exploited the economic turmoil to make money illegally. Crime and corruption are a massive problem.

A FUTURE IN THE BALANCE

Many Russians have naturally become very suspicious of the new market economy and think back to what was a more secure time in the old Soviet Union. Others are angry because the country lost territory and status when the USSR broke up. A few of these want to see a return to a tough Soviet-style Russia; others want to revive a still older Russia—that of the czars and Russian Orthodox church.

Some people fear that the economic turmoil will bring about the collapse of the Russian Federation. They think that if the non-Russian populations of the republics grow dissatisfied with Moscow's rule, they will break away from the federation. This, they say, would deepen the Russian Republic's own troubles because many of the ethnic republics have rich natural resources. The war in Chechnya (see box opposite) shows the terrible bloodshed that might arise if Moscow resists any move by the republics toward complete independence.

Russia's future hangs in the balance, and its success or failure will affect the whole world. The country's economic problems have the power to damage markets as far away as South America, and its political disintegration could create instability in Russia's neighbors, such as Ukraine, Georgia, and Kazakhstan.

People in Russia remain optimistic, however. They are prepared to work hard to make their young democracy work. Their land is rich in untapped natural resources. They have a skilled and well-educated population. They also have a lot more experience than many for surviving drastic change.

Almanac

POLITICAL

Country name:
Official form: Russian
    Federation
Short form: Russia
Local long form: *Rossiyskaya*
    Federatsiya
Local short form: *Rossiya*

Nationality:
    noun and adjective: Russian

Official language: Russian

Capital city: Moscow

Type of government: federal republic

Suffrage (voting rights):
    everyone 18 years and over

Independence: August 24, 1991

National anthem:
    from *A Life for the Czar*

National holiday:
    June 12 (Independence Day)

Flag:

GEOGRAPHICAL

Location: Northern Asia / Eastern
    Europe; latitudes 42° to 80°
    north and longitudes 28° east
    to 172° west

Climate: Dry in the south, humid in
    European Russia, and
    subarctic in Siberia.

Total area: 6,592,800 square miles
    (17,075,400 sq. km)
    land: 99%
    water: 1%

Coastline: 37,653 miles (23,396 km)

Terrain: broad plain west of Urals;
    forest and tundra in Siberia;
    mountains along southern
    borders.

Highest point: Mount Elbrus
    18,510 feet (5,642 m)
Lowest point: Caspian Sea
    -92 feet (-28 m)

Land use (1993 est.):
    permanent pastures: 4%
    arable land: 8%
    forests and woodland: 46%
    other: 42%

Natural resources: iron ore, gold, copper, nickel, lead, zinc, diamonds, gas, coal, oil

Natural hazards: volcanoes in parts

POPULATION

Population (1999 est.): 146,393,569

Population growth rate (1999 est.): -0.33%

Birthrate (1999 est.): 9.64 births per 1,000 of the population

Death rate (1999 est.): 14.96 deaths per 1,000 of the population

Sex ratio (1999 est.): 88 males per 100 females

Total fertility rate (1999 est.): 1.34 children per woman

Infant mortality rate (1999 est.): 23 deaths per 1,000 live births

Life expectancy at birth (1999 est.):
total population: 65 years
male: 59 years
female: 72 years

Literacy:
total population: 98%
male: 100%
female: 97%

ECONOMY

Currency: ruble (Rb); 1 ruble = 100 kopeks

Exchange rate (1998):
$1 = Rb20.65

Gross national product (1996):
$395 billion

Gross national product by sectors:
agriculture: 6%
industry: 41%
service: 53%

GNP per capita (1997 est.): $2,680

Average annual growth rate
(1990–1997): -7.7%

Average annual inflation rate
(1991–1998): 207.6%

Unemployment rate (1998): 11%

Exports (1997): $87.4 billion

Imports (1997): $67.6 billion

Foreign aid received: $8.5 billion

Human Development Index
(an index scaled from 0 to 100 combining statistics indicating adult literacy, years of schooling, life expectancy, and income levels):
76.9 (U.S. 94.3)

TIME LINE—RUSSIA

World History

Russian History

c. 15,000 B.C.

c. 8,000
The city of Jericho is founded.

c. 1000 B.C.

753 Traditional date of the foundation of Rome.

492–479 Wars between Persia and Greek city-states.

c. 450 Herodotus describes the Scythians—a fierce people of southern Russia.

c. 300 Sarmatians migrate to southern Russia.

c. A.D 300

306 Constantine becomes Roman emperor and legalizes Christianity.

c. 1000 Vikings land in North America.

c. 300 Slavs settle present-day Russia, Belarus, and Ukraine.

862 The Viking Rurik of Jutland becomes ruler of Novgorod.

9th–10th centuries Emergence of Kievan Rus'

1789 The French Revolution breaks out.

1775–1783 American War of Independence

1619 First African slaves arrive in Virginia.

1618 Europe rocked by the Thirty Years' War.

1520 Birth of Protestantism—the pope expels Luther from the Roman Catholic church.

1492 Columbus lands in America.

1453 Turks capture Constantinople.

1445 Gutenberg prints the first European book.

1348 Black Death breaks out in Europe.

1066 The Normans conquer Britain.

1762–1796 Catherine the Great expands the Russian empire.

1703 Peter the Great moves the capital from Moscow to St. Petersburg.

1682–1725 Peter the Great extends the Russian empire eastward into Asia.

1547 Ivan the Terrible becomes the first "Czar of All the Russias."

c. 1500

c. 1440 Ivan the Great reunites the Russian principalities.

1223 The Mongols defeat the Russian princes at the Battle of Kalka.

988 Vladimir I establishes the Russian Orthodox church.

c. 1000

c. 1800

1804 Napoleon crowns himself emperor of France.

1815 Napoleon is defeated at Waterloo.

1824 Birth of Mexican Republic

1861–1865 American Civil War

1871 Bismarck unites German states into a single country.

1812 Napoleon invades Russia, but is repelled.

1853 Russia is defeated in the Crimean War by Britain, France, and Turkey.

1861 Alexander II abolishes serfdom.

1867 Russia sells Alaska to the United States.

1868–1881 Alexander II extends Russian territory into the Caucasus and Central Asia.

2000 The West celebrates the Millennium— 2,000 years since the birth of Christ.

c. 2000

1993 Bill Clinton becomes U.S. president.

1989 Communism collapses in eastern Europe.

1963–1975 Vietnam War

1962 Cuban Missile Crisis

2000 Vladimir Putin becomes president of Russia.

1993 The Russian Federation is established.

1991 The Soviet Union collapses.

1985 Mikhail Gorbachev begins reform.

1945–1991 Cold War

c. 1950

c. 1900

1914–1918 World War I

1905 Baltic fleet destroyed in the Russo-Japanese War (1904–1905).

1905 Popular revolution breaks out across Russia.

1915 Russia joins World War I on the side of Britain and France.

1939–1945 World War II

1933 Adolf Hitler becomes German chancellor.

1945 The Red Army enters the German capital, Berlin.

1941 Germany invades Russia.

after 1925 Stalin becomes dictator.

1923 The Soviet Union (USSR) is established.

1917 Bolsheviks seize power.

c. 1918

Glossary

autonomous: Self-ruling.

Bolsheviks (Ru. "majority"):
Members of the Russian Social
Democratic Party who wanted
immediate political revolution
to overthrow the czar.

capitalism: An economic and
political system based on
trade and on individuals'
accumulation of wealth and
property—that is, capital.
Cold War, the: A long period
of tension between the USSR
and the West.
communism: A political system
in which goods and land are
owned by everyone and there
is no private property.
cossacks: Russian peasants
renowned for their riding
and fighting abilities.
coup: The overthrow
of a ruling power.
Cyrillic: A 32-letter alphabet
used for writing Russian.
czar: The title given to a
Russian ruler before the
October Revolution in 1917.

democracy: A process
that allows the people
of a country to govern
themselves, usually by voting
for a leader or leaders.
Duma, the: Part of the
Russian parliament; the
Duma's members are elected
by Russia's citizens.

exports: Goods sold by
one country to another.

free market: Term used to
describe an economy with
very little government control.
Prices are decided by the
forces of supply and demand.

glasnost' (Ru. "openness"):
A policy introduced in
conjunction with *perestroika*
by President Mikhail
Gorbachev in an attempt
to revitalize the Russian
economy.
gross national product (GNP):
Total value of goods and
services produced by the
people of a country during
a period, usually a year.
Gulag (Ru.), the: A network
of labor camps set up in 1930
by the Russian secret police.

hydroelectricity: Electricity
produced by harnessing the
water power in a river.

icons: Traditional Russian
paintings of religious figures.
Icons were usually painted on
small wooden panels
imports: Goods bought by
one country from another.
industrialized nation:
A country where manufacture
is usually carried out with the
help of machinery.

manufactured goods: Goods
ready for sale directly to the
public—for example, clothes.

Marxism: An ideology that
follows the theories of Karl
Marx. Marx believed that
capitalism will ultimately be
replaced by communism and
shared wealth.
mausoleum: A large tomb
usually used to keep the
bodies of important figures
such as a king or other leader.
mineral resources: Minerals
that can be harnessed to
provide energy or raw
materials for manufacture.
monsoon: A seasonal
summer wind that
brings heavy rainfall.

nomadic: Term used to
describe a lifestyle that
involves migration from
place to place in search
of food or shelter.

oblast (Ru.): An autonomous
province.
October Revolution, the:
A Bolshevik coup led by
Lenin that seized control of
Russia from the provisional
government. It took place
on the night of October
24–25, 1917.
okrug (Ru.): An autonomous
district.

**perestroika
(Ru. "restructuring"):**
Policy introduced alongside
glasnost' by President
Mikhail Gorbachev in an
attempt to revitalize the
Russian economy.

permafrost: Ground that is permanently frozen.
plateau: An area of level, high ground.
principality: Area of land ruled by a prince.
proportional representation: A system of election whereby political parties gain seats in parliament in proportion to the number of votes cast for them.

Russian Orthodox: A denomination of the Christian church. Russian Orthodoxy was the country's official religion under the czars, and is widely practiced today.

serfs: Russian peasants.
socialism: A political theory that teaches that society should control production rather than individuals.
steppes: Dry areas often covered in short grass; steppes receive less rain than prairies but more than deserts.

taiga: A zone of marshy forests.
treaty: An agreement signed between countries.
tundra Treeless plains in the north of Russia.

USSR (short for Union of Soviet Socialist Republics): Former communist nation made up of Russia and neighboring territories once part of the Russian empire.

vodka: A colorless alcoholic beverage popular in Russia.

Bibliography

Major Sources Used for This Book
Auty, R., and D. Obolensky, eds. *Cambridge Companion to Russian Studies*. Cambridge, U.K.: Cambridge University Press, 1976.
Figes, O. *A People's Tragedy: The Russian Revolution, 1891–1924*. New York: Penguin, 1998.
McCauley, M. *Russia, America, and the Cold War, 1949–91*. White Plains, NY: Longman Publishing Group, 1998.
Milner-Gulland, R. *The Russians*. Oxford, U.K.: Blackwell Publishers, 1999.
Serge, V. *From Lenin to Stalin*. New York: Pathfinder Press, 1973.
Dobbs, M. *Down with Big Brother: The Fall of the Soviet Empire*. New York: Vintage Books, 1994.

General Further Reading
Clawson, E. *Activities and Investigations in Economics*. Reading, MA: Addison-Wesley, 1994.
The DK Geography of the World. New York: Dorling Kindersley, 1996.
The Kingfisher History Encyclopedia. New York: Kingfisher, 1999.
Martell, H.M. *The Kingfisher Book of the Ancient World*. New York: Kingfisher, 1995.

Further Reading About Russia
Greenblatt, M. *Peter the Great and Tsarist Russia*. Rulers and Their Times. Tarrytown, NY: Benchmark Books, 2000.
Holmes, B. *Moscow*. World 100 Years Ago. Broomall, PA: Chelsea House, 1998.
Kent, D. *St. Petersburg*. Cities of the World. Danbury, CT: Children's Press, 1997.
Pozzi, G. *Chagall*. Masters of Art. New York: Peter Bedrick Books, 1997.
Vail, J. *"Peace, Land, Bread": A History of the Russian Revolution*. World History Library. New York: Facts on File, 1996.

Some Websites About Russia
www.valley.net/~transnat
virtualrussia.net

Index

Acknowledgments

Cover Photo Credits
Corbis: The Russian State Museum (Saint Cyril); Steve Raymer (Nevsky Prospekt in winter); **Duncan Brown** (St. Basil's Cathedral)

Photo Credits
AKG London: Erich Lessing 99; Duncan Brown: 36; **Corbis:** Dean Conger 22, 47, 82; W. Perry Conway 34; John Corbett; Ecoscene 24; Gianni Dagli Orti 102; Humphrey Evans: Cordaiy Photo Library Ltd 105; Wolfgang Kaehler 26, 48, 87; Steve Raymer 42, 45; Roger Ressmeyer 14; Gregor Schmid 21; The State Russian Museum 50, 98; David Turnley 90; Peter Turnley 116; **Empics:** Matthew Ashton 111; **Ronald Grant Archive:** 103; **Robert Hunt Library:** 66; **Hutchison Library:** A. Grachichenkov 91; Nick Haslam 19; Victoria Ivleva 31; Liba Taylor, 106, 112;

Leslie Woodhead 41; Andrey Zvoznikov 114; **David King Collection:** 64; **Peter Newark's Pictures:** 56, 57, 59, 61, 63, 67, 73, 84; **Novosti:** 68, 78, 101; **Tony Stone Images:** Jerry Alexander 6; James Balog 28; Demetrio Carrasco 40, 95; Natalie Fobes 33; Paul Harris 12, 30; Geoff Johnson 75; Jerry Kobalenko 96; Alain La Garsmeur 85; John Lamb 71; Siefried Layda 38; Robin Smith 44; **Werner Forman:** The Hermitage Museum St. Petersburg 52.

Text Credit
The publisher would like to thank Genia Gurarie for granting permission to reprint her translation of Pushkin's poem "The Flower" from "Pushkin: The Gabriliad and Other Poems" (senior thesis at Princeton University, 1999), which appears on p. 101.